The Naked Writer

The Naked Writer

Third Edition

BY
G. MIKI HAYDEN

Published in 2021 by JP&A Dyson
27 Old Gloucester Street, London WC1N 3AX, United Kingdom
Copyright G. Miki Hayden

https://www.jpandadyson.com

ISBN 978-1-909935-36-5

Registered with the IP Rights Office
Copyright Registration Service
Ref: 3283530718

Contents

sentence start often suppresses a great deal of life that might emerge from more imaginative word use.

We can't make statements such as, "The kids climbed all over him like their new pet." Why not? We must compare like with like. Infinitive must match infinitive, and participle must match participle.

PART II: REFINE YOUR LANGUAGE

Repetition of key or even small words, as well as word sounds, will detract from the reader's enjoyment of the language of a piece.

Not knowing the nuances of words is the most difficult problem we can contend with as writers. No absolute cure exists for this syndrome, but maybe this chapter can clarify a couple of aspects of the dilemma.

Better writers consider the rhythm of the sentences. This element is not complex in actuality, but rhythm should be a factor in our writing.

Nothing is so annoying to the reader as a disordered sentence that tends to mislead. Though English has rules for where the words should go, the rules are not as important as the logic of word order that leads to clarity.

Adjectives modify nouns, and adverbs modify verbs, adjectives, and other adverbs. So what else is new?

Our language is built for a past, present, and future and subtle variations of each. This chapter urges writers to chose the right tense and stick to it.

PART III: PUT IT TOGETHER

Quite often, the most economical way to create a sentence is to pull two or more sentences together. Conversely, we might need to cut a sentence in two or strip off the excess in order to have a manageable unit.

An admirable style eliminates the superfluous and weeds out unneeded words—sometimes even words that might be useful but that spoil the writing.

Is writing right the right way to go? Yes and no...

PART IV: MECHANICS, AKA PUNCTUATION

Punctuation changes how we read the words, but those who don't know what punctuation sounds like won't know that. That's why we all need practice in reading the pauses and emphases that punctuation adds.

Citing dialogue has almost more arcane ins and outs than the entire IRS tax code. That's why a complete chapter is needed to explain.

Most people don't know the rules of punctuation, and yet we only have a few marks with which we punctuate.

Get access to thousands of literary agents, magazines, and publishers for your work.

PART I
The Written Word

Don't Mistake This for a Beginners' Book

As if life weren't hard enough, I decided to produce a writing style/composition book. Why? On about 365 days a year I go online to check up on students in my Internet classes—only to be plagued by multiple manifestations of exactly the same mistakes that all my hundreds of other students made the previous year. Not only do many of the students have a score of identical linguistic misunderstandings in common, but those with problems repeat them endlessly, coming back to take a second and even third, progressively more advanced, class while unrepentant of their errors. Oops—I mustn't sound grouchy since I want to engage you. I tried to program macros of responses that I could insert where I found the predictable grammar, style, and punctuation glitches, but I wasn't able to make the software do what I wanted it to. What a shame, because these students really do make pretty much the same mistakes consistently; I'd love to press the F1 key, say, and have the words "OPTIONAL COMMA. DO YOU REALLY WANT A PAUSE HERE? READ IT OUT LOUD. NO, YOU DON'T" drop down into the text.

If the students in my Web-based writing classes are making the same errors time and time again, then ninety-eight percent of those writing any kind of text in this country today likely are as well. One of that immense majority could be you. (Well, if *you're* doing it, I'm sure you do it minimally and with tremendous élan.) And one of those millions of mistake-makers was surely I, at a prior point in time. I have to admit that, despite my earning a living as a writer for more than twenty years, I had no idea of many of the rules about which I nowadays nag my eager students. When I had a really fastidious copy editor go over my work, I always wondered about the enormous number of changes marked. Sheesh, how fussy some people can be.

Slowly, over time and then more quickly as I began to teach, I woke up to the actual rules (and their variations), and to the implementation of better style choices. I bought style books. I began to be irritated when others made mistakes. I forgot I had once not known the difference between "which" and "that." I wrote a rather well-received book—*Writing the Mystery, a Start-to-Finish Guide for Both Novice and Professional* (nominated for three awards, winning one)—that had a section with quite a bit of style advice. I won an Edgar for a short story of mine.

The kudos all began to go to my head. I became convinced that I could write a style book and save would-be writers of every stripe hours, days, weeks, years of agony.

So I'm the source of my own travails in writing this book.

Darn.

I hope I do save you, the reader, a bit of pain. And I'd suggest you approach the book this way: Read the text more than once, section by section, then set it aside. Now, use this book for reference when something you're writing doesn't seem to be working, or when the reaction to your writing is not a thumbs up. Learning all the rules to an admirable style doesn't happen overnight. The language, an expression of our societal and personal psyches, is just as deep as our own collective and individual intelligences.

Only as we live and learn about ourselves and about the universe we live in will our ability to communicate come to reflect our capacity to dig down, to touch our humanity, to love what is outside ourselves, and to forgive the petty sins others may commit against us. (Oh no, where did that come from? I'm sure I didn't mean to get all smarmy and philosophical on you. Forgive me. And lots of love.)

The Naked Writer Defines Terms

Words are, of course, the most powerful drug used by mankind.

—Rudyard Kipling

Adam was the first author on earth, although he didn't go around with a pad and pencil. He came into the Garden of Eden naked and soon after was asked by God to name the animals, which he did.* He made up some words, enjoyed the process a lot, and simply never stopped the obsessive naming.

What did it mean that Adam was naked? Well, obviously, he was freelance and didn't have to dress in the morning because he never left the garden until later on (Adam's leaving the garden— for New York City—came about through his compulsion to evolve, improve his writing skills, and find better markets).

Because we all come naked, speak a language, and can name a few things, we all have the potential to turn into writers. Naked writers, of course, because we have to start somewhere. Also, naked is good, because a writer ought to be without pretensions and be able to produce meaning straight from his/her original, unclothed self.

A few aspects of the business have changed since Adam's time, however, since he named a lot of items, and then his and Eve's descendents went on to name tons more stuff, both concrete and abstract. So with a great deal of the naming already done, setting down appellations has faded into the background as the primary job of the naked writer. The naked writer now has to keep in mind virtual truckloads of names, if only just for her tools. Over time, the names have been broken down into categories, in fact, since we have so darn many of them. Thus I'd best define a handful or two of basic terms that will come into play in the course of this book. Surprisingly, I don't think I'll have to clarify all that many, but hang on and I'll take a stab at it.

Parts of Speech

Notwithstanding the complexity of our English language, we have only eight different parts of speech. Having taught a grammar class repeatedly, I've been interested to note that people struggle identifying these parts of speech despite the paucity of them and in spite of the fact that we use them every day. Knowing the names of the parts of speech and understanding the function of each of the parts is fundamental for the writer, whether naked or wearing a sweater against the chill.

Nouns

Nouns stand for *things*. Things have thingness (all words ending with "ness" are nouns). Thingness can be something we can touch (concrete nouns), plus abstractions, which we can only touch with our minds (the category of which is "abstract nouns"). "Radio" is a noun, a concrete one, but so is "sleepiness" a noun, one that describes an idea, an abstraction. "Jim" is a proper noun and rates a capital at its start, while "gym" is a common noun and is lower-cased. "Gem" is a concrete noun if you show us the emerald we're talking about, but an abstract noun if you call your sweetie a gem.

Pronouns

Pronouns substitute for nouns or other pronouns. The most familiar, certainly, are the personal pronouns: *I, you, he, she, we, they, who*, and all the variations, depending on "case"—that is, how the personal pronoun is used in the sentence, such as, as a subject or an object or to claim possession—"my car." One personal pronoun we might not really think of as personal, since it doesn't relate to persons at all, is the personal pronoun "it." But "it" falls into the class defined as personal pronouns, all the same, being quite solidly known as "third person."

Indefinite pronouns refer to unspecified persons, places, or things: *anyone, each, either, no one, someone, both, few, many*, and so on. Some of these are used as singular pronouns always, some are always plural, some can be either singular or plural.** Quite a fix for a writer trying to pick out verbs or other pronouns to go with these. (*Demonstrative pronouns* are a narrower lot: *this, that, these*, and *those*.)

Since sometimes pronouns are singular and sometimes they are plural, please, please, make sure your pronouns agree in number with the antecedent for which they substitute, and make sure the verb agrees in number as well.*** Be certain you know if a pronoun is always singular, always plural, or can be either depending on use. How might you know? By looking up the word in a dictionary, either one on the Internet or a physical book you pick up and hold in your very own hands.

A couple of other categories of pronouns exist, but, good heavens, these are little words, and ever so vague, so why go into further depth in regard to them? Just try to grasp the idea of what a pronoun is. Pronouns stand in for nouns.

Verbs

Verbs minister to the nouns and pronouns. They sacrifice their own independence in order to carry the nouns here and there (to show action, even of an abstract sort) or to simply act as a link so that the concrete or abstract things (nouns/pronouns) may be modified (somehow altered or "dressed") by adjectives (defined below). Verbs serve the otherwise helpless clause subjects and have no actual agenda of their own. What admirable self-abnegation on their part! Verbs are either of an *action* or a *linking/state-of-being* type.

> ❖ *Action:* Ralph *jumped* in the river.
>
> ❖ *Linking/state-of-being:* Ralph *was* cold from swimming in the water.
>
> ❖ *Linking/state-of-being:* Ralph *felt* sick after his stupid act of bravado.
>
> ❖ *Linking/state-of-being:* Ralph *grew* nervous about the consequences of his impulsive leap.
>
> ❖ *Linking/state-of-being:* Ralph *could be* dying now and not even know it!

An action verb may be *transitive* or *intransitive*. A transitive verb takes a direct object and an intransitive verb doesn't. In the sentence "Ralph jumped in the river," the action verb "jumped" is intransitive—it has no direct object. On the other hand, if we say "Ralph jumped the fence," the verb is transitive since "fence" is the direct object.

Some verbs are always transitive, such as the verb "to hold": *I held a leaf in my hand.* The verb always has a direct object. Some verbs, such as "to sleep," are always intransitive, as they can't take a direct object. The sentences "Jane will sleep on the sofa," or "I slept for an hour" don't take direct objects. "On the sofa" and "for an hour" are both prepositional phrases that are used adverbially, as adverbs, that is. They modify the intransitive verbs.

Most action verbs sometimes take an object and sometimes don't. Therefore, we don't really have to categorize verbs as transitive and intransitive for any particular reason of making sense of the rules of language. Naming the sub-, subtype of verb is really simply an academic exercise. Just call them action verbs.

The reason we classify verbs at all is that some verbs take adverbs and some—however obedient they may be otherwise—refuse to. Linking/state-of-being verbs will not take adverbs; they link the subject with a complement—something on the other side of the verb that completes the sentence, often an adjective. The most significant linking/state-of-being verb is the "to be" verb, and to be a true linking verb, that verb generally stands on its own. That is, the "to be" form is not simply part of another verb's conjugation.

> ❖ *Linking verb:* I am his mother.
>
> ❖ *Not a linking verb:* He was beating the rug.
>
> ❖ Other linking verbs/state-of-being and sensory verbs include *feel, appear, seem, look, taste,* and so on. *The soup tastes delicious. I feel good. He appears dangerous. She looks lovely.*

In these sentences with linking verbs, the modifying complements are adjectives because the words (the adjectives) refer directly back to the subject—they are linked—and the complements modify the subject and not the verb. (Of course we can use a noun as a complement, too—"That child is a terror.")

Some of these verbs may also be used in ways that are not linking. In "I tasted the soup," for instance, the verb "taste," now an action verb, is transitive and takes an object. We can also say "I felt the wound carefully" and "I looked at her compassionately." These uses change the supposed linking verbs ("feel" and "look") to action verbs.

Moreover, sometimes verbs that seem to be linking verbs in every respect are used with an adverb or adverbial phrase, which means they aren't *actually* linking verbs.

> ❖ *Not a linking verb, but an intransitive verb*: I am here. She is at the movies.

Do you hear *The Twilight Zone* music? I feel as if I just wrote a piece for *Ripley's Believe It Or Not* on the subject of the great disappearing linking verb. I never meant to present the language in so fantastical a light. And worse is out there lurking still, though I will refrain from so much detailing ahead, I hope.

Let's turn to a little something called the verbal, and that doesn't simply mean talk, talk, talk (that's a pun, guys). *Verbals* are word types formed from verbs and consist of *gerunds*, *participles*, and *infinitives*. Gerunds and participles both may end in "ing" but serve different functions. The gerund is a noun and the participle is a modifying agent, an adjective. (The participle may also take an ending other than "ing.") The infinitive takes the basic verb, adds a "to" and gives the writer a noun, adjective, or adverb to toy with.

> ❖ *Gerund:* Digging in the garden cheered me up.
>
> ❖ *Participle:* Digging in the garden, I've found more than one fossil from the time when the sea flowed through here.

> ❖ *Participle:* The fossil dug from the garden is of a very common type.
>
> ❖ *Infinitive as a noun:* They chose to dig in the garden today.
>
> ❖ *Infinitive as an adjective:* We have dirt to dig aplenty.
>
> ❖ *Infinitive as an adverb:* I struggled to dig deeper into the soil.

That will be quite enough of verbs for now, but as humble and servile as they present themselves, this part of speech demands a lot of attention (so more to come later in the book).

Adjectives

I've used the words "adjective" and "adverb" rather freely already. What is an adjective? (As if you didn't know…) The *adjective* modifies (affects our perception of) the noun or pronoun. What is the adverb? The *adverb* modifies verbs, adjectives, and other adverbs. Both adjectives and adverbs are considered modifiers. They may have the same word root but most often take different forms. Adjectives, like other parts of speech, obviously have broken into pieces (as it were) under the Adamic naming curse and can be classified as many different types.

The three *articles*—"the," "a," and "an"—are adjectives. Typically, we use a "the" to modify an item or type of item to which we've already introduced the reader, or an item that should come as no surprise: He went into *the* kitchen and lit *the* stove. We understand he probably has a kitchen and a stove in the kitchen, and, unless he's a caterer or some such, only one kitchen and one stove. We call the "the" the *definite* article.

If the reader hasn't met the thing or creature, then we would use the "a" or "an" (*indefinite* articles): "A bird outside started to sing." If we know the bird, of course, we'd say "The bird outside started to sing."

This rule doesn't always apply with nouns that represent general quantities rather than numbered quantities (milk, for instance), which generally take a "the" (unless we're defining it as a singular: "Let's have a milk."). Oh yes, and some abstract nouns often don't take any article—"knowledge," for instance—though we can say "The knowledge I've shared with you will hold you in good stead in your career."

The "an," as we all know, is used when we're modifying an item or creature that begins with a vowel. Or is that the case? Actually we should replace the word "vowel" with "vowel sound," and say the "an" is used with a vowel sound: "Send an SASE (self-addressed, stamped envelope)." "Peel an onion." "An NKID officer, that is, an officer from the Peoples Commissariat of Foreign Affairs, reported his observations on the Eastern Front directly to Stalin."

The full scope of rules for the use of articles is mind-boggling, in fact, and I will spare you the absolute horror of it all. Suffice it to say I just saved you about seven pages of detail and a final sentence that would read something like, "Exceptions can be found."

Most students/writers do pretty well with articles, overall, except for those writers for whom English is a second language. If your English (as a second language) is excellent except for the articles, you might need to go into those arcane byways that include every rule, and you might need to scrutinize each noun you plunk down, in order to apply the correct article. But, you know what? That type of effort, if necessary for you, will pay in the long run in satisfaction and a ninety-eight percent sense of security when you submit a piece of writing at work or for publication.

Adjectives, otherwise, are not awfully problematic. Their complexity lies in the areas of comparison ("He is a more difficult person than George; in fact, he is the most difficult person I've ever met") and in deciding whether to use an adjective or adverb ("She gave a pretty smile, and I was glad she could smile so prettily").

Adverbs

Adverbs, since they are used for more purposes than adjectives— modifying one another, modifying adjectives, modifying verbs— have a few peculiar ins and outs.

I have always thought of adverbs simply as answering the question "how?" And that is pretty much the case. "How?" can mean "in what manner?" To which the answer could be "diligently" and so on. Still other questions that might be posed to elicit an adverb as

Claim your free access to **www.firstwriter.com**: *See p.263*

the response might be "when?" *Now, daily, frequently, never,* and so on are adverbs that answer the question "when?" Similarly, an adverb may answer the question of "where?" *Here, there, close, downstream, offshore,* and *far* tell us "where."

Adverbs may also account for the solution to the puzzle of "to what extent?" *More, less, further, partly, almost, very.* I shall torment you further on the topic of modifiers later on. Stay alert.

Conjunctions

The word origin of *conjunction* is the Latin "conjugare," meaning "to join together." Conjunctions join together sentence elements. The "coordinating" conjunctions are few: *and, but, or, yet, so, nor, for.* The "subordinating" conjunctions are many (*although, because, even, whereas, while*—and so on), and they are used to make a portion of the sentence subordinate to, or dependent on, the other part.

> ❖   He worked very hard because he wanted to go to college.

Here, we have two parts to the sentence, two clauses. "He worked very hard" can stand on its own, but "because he wanted to go to college" would be a fragment on its own since it doesn't form a complete sentence. We could say "He wanted to go to college" and that would stand on its own as a sentence, but the subordinating conjunction "because" turns the sentence into a subordinate or dependent clause.

Since we're defining conjunctions so carefully, we might as well mention "correlative" conjunctions as they aren't that much trouble, and since we're here. Correlative conjunctions work in pairs: *either/or, neither/nor, both/and,* and *not only/but also.* The important thing about these correlative conjunctions is that they bind the terms being joined more closely than coordinating conjunctions, and the terms being joined must be equal—for instance, both nouns or both adjectives.

❖ *Correct:* Not only will he take the girls to the movies, but he will also take the boys.

❖ *Correct:* Not only was he handsome, but also he was kind.

❖ *Incorrect:* Not only was he handsome, but he will also take the children to the movies.

Further joiners are the conjunctive adverbs, such as *otherwise, accordingly, therefore, furthermore, consequently, then, thus, also, granted, certainly, meanwhile...* As well as joining (plus comparing, contrasting, emphasizing, etc.), these types of words and phrases provide a transition from one idea to another. Because a conjunctive adverb doesn't serve the same function as a subordinating conjunction, be aware that when a conjunctive adverb joins two independent clauses, you must punctuate with more than a comma.

❖ *Incorrect:* He interviewed family and friends for the tell-all book, consequently he has more than three hundred hours on tape.

❖ *Correct:* He interviewed family and friends for the tell-all book; consequently, he has more than three hundred hours on tape.

Prepositions

Today a student of mine labeled a few random nouns and verbs as prepositions. When I asked why, he said because he didn't know what parts of speech the nouns and verbs were and because prepositions were said to show relationships. I tried to think of how to explain prepositions and this was what I came up with, for whatever the definition is worth: Prepositions often show directionality or location—toward the river, into the garden, in the street, beside the house, under the flagstone. They are basically words that don't have a lot of "life" in them, per se, but serve a function of relating other words (that is, the ideas, the things the words represent) to one another.

The object of a preposition is a noun, and the relationship shown is of the main clause to the noun that is the object of the preposition. *They flew above the clouds. The children ran across the meadow.* That is, the main clause (the subject and verb) have a relationship with the object of the preposition, and the preposition shows the kind of relationship: *under, on, over, surrounding, down, with, during, except, against, near, past,* and so on.

Interjections

Interjections should be the easiest part of speech to define. Ah! If only I could. There, the "ah" is an interjection. Why, so is the "there." And the "Why!" The interjection is a single word utterance that expresses a strong emotion—of surprise, excitement, triumph, anger, or some shade thereof. The interjection may stand on its own and be followed by an exclamation point or a question mark: What? How dare you say that? Or the interjection may be followed by a comma: Oh, I got that wrong again. Some words are only and always interjections, such as Whew! Or, gadzooks! Other words can be used as interjections in addition to another part of speech. Yes! In addition to being an interjection, "yes" can be used as a noun (*She gave him a yes*) and an adverb (*She voted yes*).

Many subclassifications of all eight parts of speech exist that most of us (me included) never heard of, all set down insidiously by the lexiconigraphic sons and daughters of the original, happy-go-lucky Adam himself.

Phrases and Clauses

Right after parts of speech in our glossary must come the terms *phrases* and *clauses.* These units of expression represent one level up from the single word, and understanding them is essential to our comprehending how we form sentences (and the rules of punctuation).

A *clause* has at least a subject and a verb, but may have other elements, such as modifiers and objects. The subject (that which is under primary consideration) will generally be present—but may be absent. In the imperative sentence "Hand me that letter," the subject (you) is understood—but doesn't actually appear. ("Me" is not the subject because it is the object.)

A clause may be *independent*, which means that the clause itself forms a sentence on its own, or *dependent* (subordinate), which means that some provisional element, usually a subordinating conjunction, keeps the clause from standing alone as a sentence.

> ❖ *Independent clause/subordinate clause:* You owe me money since I paid for your cab.
>
> ❖ *Independent clause:* You owe me money.
>
> ❖ *Subordinate clause:* ...since I paid for your cab.
>
> ❖ *Independent clause:* I paid for your cab.
>
> ❖ *Subordinate clause/independent clause:* Since you owe me money, I'd like it back.

If you feel confused by this, ignore the whole topic while simply letting your eyes take in the words. Don't struggle with anything that doesn't strike you as readily understandable. Let the definitions flow by and just try to remember the key words. I don't mean for you to work too hard with any of this. Remember, this is also a reference book, and if you really need the information later on, you can come back to it. Let your mind work as it will; force won't help. You'll understand eventually as you relax and allow the concepts to cook their way through the synapses of your capable and intelligent brain. Really.

A *phrase* is a logical grouping of words that doesn't have both a subject and a verb. The phrases below begin with a preposition and are called *prepositional phrases*. The prepositional phrase can be used for transition, as an adverb phrase, and as an adjective phrase.

> ❖ Transitional phrase: as a result

❖ Adverb phrase: before the weekend

❖ Adjective phrase: with more than enough spicy flavors.

We may also use verbs to create other parts of speech (as mentioned above, under "verbs") and then to form phrases, such as "winding his way through the forest." This type of formation can be a noun (as a gerund). In "He caught heck from his mother for letting out the dog," the word "letting" is fashioned from the verb "let" and is now a noun used in the prepositional phrase "for letting out the dog."

In "Winding his way through the forest, James thought he heard the cough of a foraging dragon," the "winding" is a participle formed from "wind" and used here to create an adjective phrase that modifies "James."

Again, don't worry about any of this. If you've read the words, you've done your job so far. Just remember "phrases" and "clauses."

* NB (*nota bene*, which means *note well*): Mark Twain, an author who wore a suit and smoked a pipe, says that Eve did the naming, and perhaps he was right, because, in the Garden, Adam and Eve were actually one unitary creature. Who could tell the two, joined at the hip as they were, apart?

**Also NB, the commas here separate independent clauses. Note well that the clauses are short; otherwise, note well, I would use semicolons to separate them.

*** "…make sure the verb agrees in number" is an independent clause. What's the subject? The "mood" expressed is *imperative* and the subject is "you," a word that is taken as understood. The reason I point out that this is an independent clause is in order to explain the comma before the "and." The "and," here, joins two independent clauses. Often, writers habitually use a comma before coordinating conjunctions joining a dependent clause to an independent clause. Don't do that habitually. Sometimes, however, you may *choose* to use the comma. My, my, what a complex language.

Quiz

Part I.

Name the parts of speech for the numbered words:

She is munching (1) on a scone (2) laden (3) with Devonshire cream at high tea in Manhattan's Plaza Hotel—all eighty-nine (4) pounds of her—while in the background (5) a harpsichordist plays Chopin. Nearby (6), a table of private school girls, demure (7) in cashmere and red velvet, celebrate (8) a birthday.

"If I make a lot of money…" author Lynda Sandoval (9) begins. She pauses and corrects (10) herself, "*When* (11) I make a lot of money…"

She isn't being (12) show-offy (13), but radiates a hopeful and self-assured innocence. The money, she already knows, is going to come, and, anyway (14), she definitely (15) wants to choose the more positive (16) statement. She has been through a lot in her career and has hung (17) in steadily during the tough times. The good times are just about to roll (18).

Sitting (19) here, the petite Sandoval is on the verge of being introduced to the world as the Latina (20) author who (21) is going to make it big in women's fiction. Her breakthrough book, for (22) which she was paid an unspecified six figure advance, will be celebrated in three days' time—along with Sandoval herself— at a grand party in Manhattan, an (23) event co-sponsored (24) by *People Magazine en Espanol* and Sandoval's publisher, HarperCollins (the Rayo imprint). Film rights have been bid on and (25) the press is already clamoring at the happy-faced author's door.

Part II.

Which are independent clauses? Which are dependent clauses? Which are phrases?

1. Book Expo America (BEA) convenes workers
2. in the vineyards
3. of the printed word,
4. and this year because it was held in New York City's Javitts

Center
5. traveling as it does
6. from L.A., to Chicago, to New York
7. I was able to attend.
8. And lo and behold, BEA was simply, just, another trade show.
9. Not that I don't like trade shows,
10. because I actually do.
11. And I think that for the writer,
12. the trade show of our industry is a good place to spend a couple of hours or even a couple of days hanging out.
13. When they say the show has two thousand exhibits,
14. you have to bear in mind that this is a booksellers' show,
15. so many of the products displayed are items bookstores also sell (bookmarks) or need (bookcases) and which literary people could care less about.
16. Remember, also,
17. that many of the exhibits represent oddball areas
18. of (little) interest
19. with a single person manning a lonely booth,
20. wondering if anyone will bother to drop by
21. (no one does).

Answers

Part I.

She is munching (1 *verb*) on a scone (2 *noun*) laden (3 *past participle/adjective*) with Devonshire cream at high tea in Manhattan's Plaza Hotel—all eighty-nine (4 *adjective*) pounds of her—while in the background (5 *noun*) a harpsichordist plays Chopin. Nearby (6 *adverb*),a table of private-school girls, demure (7 *adjective*) in cashmere and red velvet, celebrate (8 *verb*) a birthday.

"If I make a lot of money…" author Lynda Sandoval (9 *proper noun*) begins. She pauses and corrects (10 *verb*) herself, "*When* (11 *adverb*) I make a lot of money…"

She isn't being (12 *adjective/participle*) show-offy (13 *adjective*), but radiates a hopeful and self-assured innocence. The money, she already knows, is going to come, and, anyway (14 *adverb*), she definitely (15 *adverb*) wants to choose the more positive (16 *adjective*) statement. She has been through a lot in her career and has hung (17 *verb*) in steadily during the tough times. The good times are just about to roll (18 *infinitive as adverb*).

Sitting (19 *participle as adjective*) here, the petite Sandoval is on the verge of being introduced to the world as the Latina (20 *adjective*) author who (21 *pronoun*) is going to make it big in women's fiction. Her breakthrough book, for (22 *preposition*) which she was paid an unspecified six figure advance, will be celebrated in three days' time—along with Sandoval herself—at a grand party in Manhattan, an (23 *article/adjective*) event co-sponsored (24 *participle/ adjective*) by *People Magazine en Espanol* and Sandoval's publisher, HarperCollins (the Rayo imprint). Film rights have been bid on and (25 *coordinating conjunction*) the press is already clamoring at the happy-faced author's door.

Part II.

Which are independent clauses? Which are dependent clauses? Which are phrases?

1. Book Expo America (BEA) convenes workers (*independent clause*)
2. in the vineyards (*phrase*)
3. of the printed word, (*phrase*)
4. and this year because it was held in New York City's Javitts Center (*dependent clause*)
5. traveling as it does (*dependent participle clause used as an adjective*)
6. from L.A., to Chicago, to New York (*phrases*)
7. I was able to attend. (*independent clause*)
8. And lo and behold, BEA was simply, just, another trade show. (*independent clause*)
9. Not that I don't like trade shows, (*independent clause*)
10. because I actually do. (*dependent clause*)

11. And I think that for the writer, (*dependent clause*)
12. the trade show of our industry is a good place to spend a couple of hours or even a couple of days hanging out. (*independent clause*)
13. When they say the show has two thousand exhibits, (*dependent clause*)
14. you have to bear in mind that this is a booksellers' show, (*independent clause*)
15. so many of the products displayed are items bookstores also sell (bookmarks) or need (bookcases) and which literary people could care less about. (*dependent clause*)
16. Remember, also, (*independent clause*)
17. that many of the exhibits represent oddball areas (*dependent clause*)
18. of (little) interest (*phrase*)
19. with a single person manning a lonely booth, (*phrase*)
20. wondering if anyone will bother to drop by (*dependent participle clause*)
21. (no one does). (*independent clause without the parentheses*)

Where Do Words Come From, Mommy?

No one knows, child. No one knows…

"The roots of language are irrational and of a magical nature."

—Jorge Luis Borges
Prologue to "El otro, el mismo"

"When William Caxton set up the first printing press in England and began to mass produce books in English, he had to make decisions about how to set words on paper with his radical new technology. He decided to use as his base one of the many dialects found in England at the time. Consequently, he spelt the word for a navigable, inland body of water a lake, rather than lak or even loch, both of which were also in common use. Most later printers followed Caxton's lead, including many Scottish printers, resulting in a major new direction in the evolving process of standardizing English spelling."

—Daniel Kies
Department of English, College of DuPage, Glen Ellyn, IL

Even apes have a language—what species doesn't, whether we can personally interpret it or not? (Do use a question mark with a rhetorical question, dear friends—or an exclamation point.) Probably half our words in English aren't from Olde English, Latin, or French, but are from the language of some prehistoric hominid tribe. (I lie.) However, a branch of linguistics, etymology, delves into the question of where words originate. A few examples follow of how we know nothing of the origins of words and how silly even wondering about such tenuous considerations is. (Oh, hell, wondering never costs more than a few hours' time and an Internet connection.)

From whence comes the word "honeymoon"?

One theory is that in Babylonia four thousand years ago, for a lunar month after the wedding, the bride's father would supply his son-in-law with all the mead or honey beer he could drink. Hence, honeymoon. No? Well, how about the other theory, that "honey" refers to the sweetness of a new marriage and "moon" implies that the couple's happiness will wane? Another guess is that the derivation is German or Irish because in both cultures a newly married couple would drink an alcoholic beverage made of honey brew every night for a month, ensuring fertility and joy.

How about the expression "mind your P's and Q's"?

In English pubs, brew is ordered by pints and quarts, and in the old days the barkeep would yell out at customers getting a bit rambunctious, "Mind your pints and quarts, and quiet down." Okay, if that seems too silly, maybe the expression comes from the schoolroom, where children are apt to confuse the lowercase "p" with the lowercase "q." Or maybe the expression does originate in the tavern, where a running tally of drinks was kept behind the bar for later payment, and a customer was warned to mind how the barman chalked down the order.

How about the word "golf "?

The rumor is that when a new game was invented many years ago in Scotland, the sign went up in front of the establishment where it was played: Gentlemen Only...Ladies Forbidden. And thus was coined the sport's name—"golf." According to another source, however, women were only discouraged from playing golf later on, in Victorian times. So other opinions about the word have prevailed. The name may come from the medieval Dutch word "kolf " or "kolve," which meant "club." The word then passed to the Scots, whose old Scots dialect transformed the word into "golve," "gowl," or "gouf."

So you see, a lot of big apes got together and said, "Let's say something different. Let's talk English." And they did.

Actually, we don't know how any particular language originated, but inevitably man began to chatter about this and that— first about the tribe of thugs over the hill and "our" defense against "them," and next thing, what they were going to have for dinner. Thus, words are old.

A recent article in *The New York Times* discussed the new lexographers, a bunch of babies editing the dictionaries that record and reflect, and actually codify our everyday language. Yes, babies —very young people who weren't around when the original words were invented, and who have no right to now be in charge of what we say. Oh well, what can we do? But they seem to be erasing the archaic words from their books, and thus when authors go to replicate the speech of characters and historic figures from the eighteenth and nineteenth centuries, we will only get: "Yes, like, man, prithee go forth."

But that's bound to happen. Look at it this way—we've lost all the info we accumulated during pre-sand Egypt and have since had to start over from scratch in terms of knowledge—never quite getting up to snuff again, I might add.

Just as we can't figure out where language comes from, we don't know where the language is to go. Language transforms with the culture.

Our language today has to cope with an influx of a great many new words because of enormous changes in technology in the last number of years. Science and industry are fleet of foot in chasing their profit, but the lexographers, even the babies who have been hired to edit the Big Books, are not quite that quick off the mark.

First of all, bringing out a new dictionary takes a while. I can imagine the editors at the dictionary publishers having weekly meetings to heatedly discuss the possibility of adding new words. I'm sure we've all been at similar meetings, too—pass the Advil. (The word Advil is trademarked, you know. A word! Trademarked!)

Do we write "cellphone"? Or do we write "cell phone"? I just checked a database of multiple dictionaries, and "cell phone" had seven hits with two computer dictionary responses and one definition in an automotive dictionary. By comparison, "cellphone" got four general matches and one computing dictionary match. Yet word on the street, among writers, is that "cellphone" is being advocated by the editors.

What to do? I guess I can't simply say "use the dictionary," can I? But, do use the dictionary, and then use your own sense of propriety for any of these questions left unanswered. After that, accept the preference of the editor if the writing is for publication—or of your boss, so you don't get in Dutch (an interesting expression, that—and the question is whether to cap the "d"—yes).

Gender and the Pronoun

One major fuss in recent years—and the controversy dragged on for a ridiculously long time—was over the question of gender and pronouns—his or her, he/she, their, and the like. The absolute conclusion has finally been drawn. I guess an official grammarian, licensed like the lexographers noted above, made a final decision. Oh, the lexographers aren't licensed? That means decisions are usually up to you and me. *Carumba* (not only a foreign language exclamation, but the name of a typesetter's font).

The main thing to now know is that we can now use a plural pronoun when the rules of grammar insist on a singular.

❖ *Breakthrough and correct pronoun match:* When you go to the doctor, ask them to check your blood cholesterol. *I wasn't brought up this way, but here we are.*

❖ *Correct match:* When you go to the doctor, ask him or her to check your blood cholesterol. *You can say this if you must, but I suppose it's out of date.*

❖ *Correct match:* When you go to the doctor, ask her to check your blood cholesterol.

❖ *Correct match:* When you go to the doctor, ask him to check your blood cholesterol.

Of course if we use the "him," readers will think we're sexist—unless we're rotating the use of him and her throughout an article or book or unless we're clear about the person we're referring to.

The problem for us isn't with usage when the language has officially moved on and can be verified by looking up the correct application, but when American English is in the process of transformation. Again, that progression may take quite a while to complete itself, and with a flood of questions up for grabs, we have to wing it in our writing, hoping to avoid looking stupid.

Here are a couple of language points that have been in process for the last thirty or more years. Or might we say that these refuse to change from the form they always took, although a group of philistines keeps pushing to alter what the righteous know as absolutely "correct"? Remember, in matters of language, correct is what the culturally anointed (Strunk and White, William Safire, and so on) determine to be the standard usage.

Raise vs. Rear

I used to mark students on this one, but I've given up. The saying in the old days went, "Chickens are raised and children are reared." This aphorism may still hold true, but most common folk don't adhere to that sense of the difference. Perhaps "reared" sounds rude or awkward, but the word has lost favor. However, we will always find a person or two who will look at the word "raised" when applied to humans and snort.

Not wanting to be caught on the ignorant end of the stick or misunderstood, I use the term "brought up" when discussing the rearing of a person or persons. "He was brought up in Illinois" will most often work without the grunt, groaning, sniffing, or other sound effects. Bear in mind, we can generally find a workaround to any usage that seems ill defined or potentially wrong.

All Right vs. Alright

"Alright" is listed in thirteen dictionaries on the database I use, even though the notation warns that the spelling is nonstandard. Nonstandard in regard to dictionary use, that is. I spell it "all right" because "they" make me do it (I don't mind), but the standard spelling I see from students is "alright." Remember the old saying, "You can't fight city hall"? I think that applies here. (I do mark my students' spelling with a sigh.) Use the "all right" and you can't go wrong. Except with an editor who doesn't know her p's and q's, and in actual experience (another sad sigh), you'll find many. (If I could only tell tales... But I won't.)

The language we use in our day-to-day speech and writing is complex, deep, convoluted, and alive. As the world around us changes and as new people with a different set of perceptions begin to take charge of how we can express ourselves, revisions are made to our common lingo and its applications. Often the old disappears completely and we can search for a word we recall from 19th century literature and it's (sob) gone. As with everything else around us, we ought to keep up in order to take advantage of the latest and greatest, and so we can continue to find a niche in contemporary life. The language actually changes less than many other things we have to deal with today and does so more slowly, so we have time to adjust.

On the other hand, in the few months that JP&A Dyson (blessed be its name) will need to get this book into print, a few grammatical rules and preferences might go entirely topsy turvy. Thus, if you see anything in here you think is incorrect, believe me, it isn't. The supposed goof must be a result of the lexographers pulling out the rug from under us. This book's editor and I are never wrong. We were wrong once in 1982, but that was an inserted typo. Trust us. And just in case, double-check with two or three additional sources. That's what I do.

Exercise

Part I.

Look up the origins of the following words or phrases:

1. Limelight
2. Hell in a handbasket
3. The bee's knees
4. A lot of irons in the fire
5. Wheeling and dealing
6. The whole nine yards
7. America
8. Blackmail
9. Thinking outside the box

10. The buck stops here

Part II.

Define the following:

1. BTW
2. Viropause
3. Tuckerism
4. Bobo
5. Wingnut
6. Pleather
7. Woofys
8. Metrosexual
9. Geekalicious

Answers

Part I.

1. *Limelight*—The mineral, lime, was used to make a spotlight employed on the stage in England during Victorian times.
2. *Hell in a handbasket*—The expression could be from the French Revolution, when heads cut off at the guillotine were then carried away in a handbasket. Or this could be from the time of the building of the U.S. transcontinental railroad, when Chinese workers were lowered in a wicker chair over the side of a cliff to set a dynamite charge. Some returned to the top; some didn't.
3. *The bee's knees*—This expression for an especially good thing comes from the fact that the honeybee collects pollen in receptacles on the mid-section of its hind legs.
4. *A lot of irons in the fire*—Blacksmiths could only work iron that was red hot and thus malleable (still true today, but we don't have quite as many blacksmiths), so the smiths would place the ironwork in the fire for shaping later on. A busy blacksmith would have a lot of irons in the fire.
5. *Wheeling and dealing*—The term seems to come from the old West, where a wheeler-dealer was a gambler who played both the roulette table and cards.
6. *The whole nine yards*—Nine yards was the length of an ammunition belt used on machine guns during World War

II. In looking this up, you probably found a bunch of other interesting conjectures though.

7. *America*—The name honors navigator Amerigo Vespecci (or, Alberigo Vespucci), who claimed to have discovered the North American continent. How true this man's stories of his journeys were is uncertain, as he recanted part of his tale at the time of his death.

8. *Blackmail*—The "mail" in blackmail apparently derives from an old Scottish word for "rent." The term refers possibly to the protection racket carried out against farmers of the time, or to the undervaluing by landowners of the produce the farmers paid as their rent, or perhaps to the kidnapping of the farmers' sheep for ransom.

9. *Thinking outside the box*—The expression is a fairly recent one and might refer to a classic puzzle that requires the solver to connect nine dots using four lines without lifting pen from paper. The nine dots form a box and, apparently, the puzzle can't be solved without going outside the box.

10. *The buck stops here*—Some card games use a marker called a "buck" to show which player is acting as the current dealer. When the buck is passed to the next player, the responsibility for dealing is passed along with it. The phrase "The buck stops here" was popularized by Harry S. Truman when he was president.

Part II.

1. *BTW*—That's Internet talk for "by the way."
2. *Viropause*—The point at which male virility ends. (Oh oh, I've scared some folks.)
3. *Tuckerism*—The use of the name of a friend or a famous person for a character in fiction.
4. *Bobo*—Bobo as an adjective can mean cheap quality—such as "bobo toothpaste," but the more generally accepted meaning is bourgeois bohemian.
5. *Wingnut*—This is a noun or an adjective and is used to mean an extremist who is not mentally stable.
6. *Pleather*—This is a plastic fabric made to look like leather.
7. *Woofys*—Well off older folks. I'd spell the word "woofies," if I had the choice.

8. *Metrosexual*—A straight urban guy fussy about his appearance and in touch with his feminine side. The antonym (sort of) is"retrosexual," a heterosexual man who is basically a slob.

9. *Geekalicious*—An adjective for a person or thing who is a geek but/and delicious.

Clarity Is Job One

—Albert Camus
Writer and philosopher (1913–1960)

We could go on, day and night, thinking our own muddled thoughts or having our fragmentary fantasies, and likely be entirely happy with the quality of our reflections. We'd understand our own chaotic musings to the nth degree, or at least to the extent we each consider necessary.

In placing ideas on paper or on screen, however, our aim is usually far different from the intention (or lack of it) behind random introspection. Above all, whatever our purpose in writing a memo, a story, a news report, or a college paper, we aren't doing the work solely for our own consumption. Unless we're keeping a diary or journal (a popular thing to do these days), we intend for one or more other people to read what we've written.

That's why what we set down on paper must be absolutely clear—because we're reaching out to the external world with our words. We have to emerge from our personal dream space for a bit and enter into the perspective of the reader. Although we may not construct our prose in order to *please* the reader, we still have to imagine his or her viewpoint and knowledge—or lack of knowledge—of our topic, vocabulary, and phrasing. If we remain completely self-absorbed, the writing we do will not come across as well as we'd like. Writing, after all, is communication and not a one-way street. Therefore, when we craft that essay, short story, or work report, we should direct our minds to monitoring from a cognitive stance a bit distanced from our usual one. We need to understand what readers will experience when they take in our words.

Our job is to be objectively clear and exacting in every nuance of every sentence we produce. (Relax—the job of sentence architect is actually fun.)

In fact, clarity is our first obligation in pulling together ideas to transmit electronically or to put into print. Clarity means we will make the writing accessible to anyone able to read the English language—or, more precisely, we make the writing comprehensible for the entire grouping of our specific, chosen audience.

Thus if we are writing a young adult book, the slant we take in our use of words and with our material will be inclined toward the fourteen-year-old reader. If we don't know at this time what that mindset is like, we'd better find out. Approaching our task from this readership's point of view might mean research among any fourteen-year-old consumers we happen to know. Or our intelligence gathering may take us to the young adult corner of a local bookstore.

Being clear for those in this age group means we can't assume they know how a ribbon was used on a manual typewriter. (Maybe some of *us* don't know, either.) In writing our story set in the 1920s—or perhaps a history of World War II for eighth graders—we may have to explain how the ribbon was used. In this way, we make the story accessible by monitoring what we write as if we *were* that fourteen-year-old child. We are clear, then, in addressing our selected audience.

Be Specific

To begin with, in being clear in our writing, we can't allow any vague elements or implications that are not directly on target to our intended meaning. And we can't tell ourselves that "the reader will understand," because the reader's job is *not* to bridge the gap between the words set on the page and the meaning. The reader has another responsibility ahead—processing what we've said, rather than decoding the statement itself.

Let's look at what being specific might mean in concrete terms.

> ❖ *Vague:* Other people he did business with would honestly forget how much work they'd commissioned.
>
> ❖ *Specific:* Some of his clients would simply forget how much work they'd commissioned.

Changing "other people" to "some clients" may seem like a minor transformation, but when we do this, the reader can better understand the relationship being discussed.

> ❖ *Vague*: We hiked toward the trailer park, where we soon came upon a blue and white one.
>
> ❖ *Specific*: We hiked toward the trailer park, where we soon came upon a blue and white motor home.

The idea here is to fill in what we're talking about and not lazily allow the reader to deduce the facts. The original sentence, moreover, is the key to why we have to say "trailer" or "motor home" and can't leave in the word "one." In the first version, as written, we don't refer to trailers in the proposition part of the sentence. We say "trailer park," instead. So when we come to the word "one," we're really referring to a trailer park, not a trailer. That construction doesn't work to convey the meaning—which is that we found a particular trailer. We could say, though: "We hiked among the trailers, where we soon came upon a blue and white one." This also implies the importance of parallel construction, which we'll discuss later on in the book.

> ❖ *Not specific:* She dried her short, professionally cropped red hair.
>
> ❖ *Specific:* She dried her red hair, which was cut in a short, professional-looking style.

Here, in sentence one, we might be trying to say that a professional had cut the woman's hair. Sometimes, as writers, we'll see a meaning in what we set down, even though the words don't support the connotations we have in mind. We have to train ourselves to look at our own language from an objective point of view, with a clear mind. (If only we could look at all of life that way.) We can't assume that we're making a particular statement without first checking that the meaning is actually articulated.

Be Exact

In order for us to be perfectly clear, our statements have to be made with an eye to the *precise* meaning of each element. We can't pretend that words mean what we *want* them to mean, or that simply because the whole will be understood, the elements don't have to be sculpted with a concern for the explicit meaning of each bit. For instance:

> ❖ *Not exact:* The science building is in the middle of the three large ones.
>
> ❖ *Exact:* The science building is the center one in the grouping of three.

Obviously, the science building isn't in the middle of any other buildings at all, although a physics building might have its oddball tricks. The writer's job is to render an entirely accurate representation of the world conceived and/or described.

> ❖ *Not exact:* My desk is piled high with reports and appraisals, not to mention the stack of phone calls.
>
> ❖ *Exact:* My desk is piled high with reports and appraisals, and I have a stack of phone messages to address.

The phone calls aren't stacked, but the message slips are.

> ❖ *Not exact:* His strategy to cross over the Rappahannock River was delayed by a pontoon train.

> ❖ *Exact:* The movement of troops over the Rappahannock River to carry out Burnside's strategy was delayed by a pontoon train.

His strategy isn't delayed, because "strategy" is an idea. What is delayed is the carrying out of his strategy. What is delayed is the movement of troops.

Awkward Wording

Fulfilling our goal of being clear in writing also encompasses many other types of issues, such as using clear rather than awkward wording.

> ❖ *Awkward phrasing:* Maybe her professor's behavior was disquieting just to her.
>
> ❖ *Clearer phrasing:* Maybe she had misperceived her professor's behavior as sexual harassment.

The original, awkwardly worded phrase doesn't take into account how readers' minds work. That is, readers will begin to try to figure out the meaning of the cryptic sentence, which will distract them from the material itself. More explanation of what is being said is needed.

> ❖ *Awkward phrasing:* The corn field turned quickly into woods as we made our way along the path. The air changed from a hot, dry feeling, to cool and pine-scented.
>
> ❖ *Clearer phrasing:* The corn field turned quickly into woods as we made our way along the path. The hot, dry air became cool and pine scented.
>
> ❖ *Even clearer phrasing:* After traversing the corn field, we crossed quickly into the woods. The hot, dry air

> became cool and pine scented.
> (Note that the compound adjective doesn't take a
> hyphen unless it's in front of the noun.)

Those of us who are native speakers convey certain concepts in specific, fixed ways. If the idea is expressed in words phrased differently than the norm ("the air changed from a hot, dry feeling"), the reader will not be able to understand directly without having to first "translate" in some way. Again, this action of making sense of the text is not the reader's properly apportioned task.

Note also with the above that the corn field certainly doesn't turn into woods. That would require divine intervention. But, nonetheless, we do frequently employ this type of expression, which is not considered incorrect. That we accept one illogical phrase and throw out the second might seem arbitrary and unfair. Indeed, in some respects, the language, as a whole, can appear to be a capricious hodgepodge—as I've examined in the first couple of chapters of this book. We can't do anything about that problem, and we'll never find an ultimate judge who will adequately address our language complaints. But if we want to write in a better-than-readable style for the public, we'll have to stick to a sensible middle path, bending logic in some common instances, while cleaving strictly to the rational in others—every time according to accepted use. However, the strictest minds (yes, I mean *people* whose thinking processes operate in obedience to sound reasoning) will take an approach in writing that, to the extent possible, leaves not one shred of the sentence in doubt. Hallelujah.

Word Placement

> ❖ *Unclear:* He is a little older than I am—at forty-two.
>
> ❖ *Clear:* At forty-two, he is a little older than I.

Here, simply changing the position of the words brings the meaning into focus.

Missing Words

> ❖ *Incomplete:* But I had made a promise when I married Jack and couldn't break that vow to run off with another man.
>
> ❖ *Complete:* But I had made a promise when I married Jack and couldn't break that vow in order to run off with another man.

Again, the readers may well know what the first sentence means and will correct their interpretation a millisecond after misreading it, but we don't want to lead them astray, even for that long. While this type of picky, fussy correction might seem extreme, the truth is that careful writing can be just as much fun for the reader as careless writing—the fun in the material depends on content. And writing that sticks to splitting linguistic hairs will help that one reader who counts the most—you, when you read over your paper, which is already in your professor's hands, and go, "Oh, no, what did I say?"

> ❖ *Incomplete:* The clock radio's red light of 6:34 a.m. told me I was running late.
>
> ❖ *Complete:* The clock radio's red-lit numerals announcing 6:34 a.m. told me I was running late.

This is also a form of being specific. Specifically, the red light illuminates the *numbers* and the numbers are the element that provides the time.

Wrong Word

> ❖ *Wrongly Worded:* He found the sight of her crawling about in the mud undignified and absurd.

> ❖ *Correctly Worded:* He found her crawling about in the mud undignified and absurd.

The sight isn't undignified, but her action is.

> ❖ *Wrongly Worded:* Rules against any kind of open flame in the lab are undeniable.
>
> ❖ *Correctly Worded:* Rules against any kind of open flame in the lab must be obeyed.

In many cases, incorrect wording has to do with poor vocabulary skills. A dictionary can help, but reading is probably one of the best exercises for the development of a good vocabulary. Reading allows the writer to see how words are used and what the nuance of each word is. This isn't to say that everything in print is flawless, but a discriminating choice of reading material can help by providing the better models of not only vocabulary, but writing technique as well.

Hard-to-follow Negative

> ❖ *Confusing:* I'll not pretend this isn't frightening.
>
> ❖ *Clear:* I find this frightening.

While the first version may seem more elegantly worded than the second, the use of two negatives is confusing and might cause readers to have to stop and decide if the event is frightening or not. Negatives can be confusing, whether they are correct, as in the example above, or incorrect, as in the use of a double negative intending a single negation only ("It don't matter none to me"). Sometimes, however, such an intended double negative use helps to make a subtle point that couldn't be made if the wording was less confusing. For instance, "I didn't want her to not go, simply because I said so." That would not necessarily translate into, "I wanted her to go." We should be guided to a great extent by the desire to write in a straightforward and clear fashion, but, more importantly, we want to communicate shades of meaning with as much exactitude as possible.

Incomplete Ideas

Sometimes material is confusing not because of the words used or the way they are placed in the sentence, but because the idea hasn't been stated in its entirety. The idea being expressed has to be completed as the statement is made. The concept can be amplified later, but the initial statement has to contain all the elements needed for an immediate, clear understanding.

❖ *Incomplete:* They know more about us than our own government.

❖ *Complete:* They know more about us than our own government does.

If the thought isn't completed, the sentence could read as "They know more about us than they know about our government." Even if this seems like a silly interpretation, strictly speaking we ought to be quite clear as to what we're saying. Because, if we're not, as sure as God made little green apples, at least one reader is going to take the sentence in the wrong way. At any rate, when we read a sentence that isn't quite complete, we feel that something is amiss. As writers, we don't want to arouse that sense of unease in the reader.

❖ *Incomplete:* In her state, she didn't notice when John entered the room.

❖ *Complete:* In her state of distraction, she didn't notice when John entered the room.

Or we can first describe her distraction and then say, "In that state, she didn't notice when John entered the room."

> ❖ *Incomplete:* I'm usually his favorite target, so it was nice to have him thinking about someone else.
>
> ❖ *Complete:* I'm usually his favorite target, so it was nice to have him thinking about someone else for a change.

Waiting for the completion of the sentence is like waiting for the other shoe to drop. We don't want to make the reader wait in vain.

Another way of failing to complete our expression of the idea has to do with simply not giving enough information. In this type of situation, the added element that finalizes the meaning for us might not have to be conveyed within the sentence itself, but can be stated nearby.

> ❖ *Incomplete:* Knowing that if he staggered and fell, John was at his side to catch him, made the humiliation of being helped like an invalid barely endurable.
>
> ❖ *Complete:* Knowing that if he staggered and fell, John was at his side to catch him, made the humiliation of being helped like an invalid barely endurable. He could not stand for John to see him this way.
>
> ❖ *Or:* Knowing that if he staggered and fell, John was at his side to catch him, made the humiliation of being helped like an invalid somewhat endurable. John was the only one whose help he could tolerate.

Unless the idea is completed, we don't know if John's help makes the situation better or worse.

Exercise

Part I.

The best way to cultivate clarity is by locating its opposite. Since you probably can't pinpoint your own lack of clarity (if you could, you would have already corrected it), you'll have to choose someone else's writing to pick on.

Take some time not only to read some chosen work, but to acknowledge what you feel is unclear in the material. Usually, in order to continue on, we simply gloss over what we don't comprehend, trying to get the gist of what is said. But what you need to do for this practice is focus on the sentences that are confusing.

Now, correct the flawed sentences yourself—in writing. Try using your local newspaper as a source. Because the news goes into print quickly, more careless errors can be found in the newspaper than in books (hopefully). You can also mark the questionable sentences in red as you go because the paper was only headed to the recycling bin, anyway.

By clarifying someone else's work, you've brought your attention to these issues. This will help you view your own writing in a new and more objective way.

Don't try this exercise only once, but work at it from time to time, until you think in terms of clarity when you both read and write.

Part II.

Clarify the following sentences. Revise in any way necessary.

1. What should I pack for the trip? Nothing I don't want to lose, like my books.
2. The Saudis have been buying real estate in Little Italy for years. Not only here but around the country.
3. Different people were having different conversations at the same time.
4. Richard continued to stare into the dark, holding onto the moment compressed by urgent necessity.
5. The highlight of the concert was when the band retired backstage.
6. Jack turned his head down.
7. In his personal pantheon of memories, Larry imagined himself putting a trash bag filled with images and experiences involving his worst days out on the sidewalk for pickup.
8. The only problem in getting out of here was not being noticed.
9. The conversation of this group lacked logical succession.

10. My concern about most of these people did not weigh too heavily because they were out of their element.

Answers

Part II.

Your own change may be good, but here are some suggested changes:

1. What should I pack for the trip? Nothing I don't want to lose, like my books.
   I won't pack anything, such as my books, that I don't want to lose.
2. The Saudis have been buying real estate in Little Italy for years. Not only here but around the country.
   The Saudis have been buying real estate in New York City's Little Italy for years. They've also bought other property around the country.
3. Different people were having different conversations at the same time.
   Many little groupings of people held their own private conversations at the same time.
4. Richard continued to stare into the dark, holding onto the moment compressed by urgent necessity.
   Richard continued to stare into the dark, desperately holding on to the moment.
5. The highlight of the concert was when the band retired backstage.
   The highlight of the concert was the encore, after which the band retired backstage.
6. Jack turned his head down.
   Jack looked at the ground.
7. In his personal pantheon of memories, Larry imagined himself putting a trash bag filled with images and experiences involving his worst days out on the sidewalk for pickup.
   Larry sorted through his memories and imagined himself putting out for pickup a trash bag filled with his worst experiences.

8. The only problem in getting out of here was not being noticed.
   The only problem he might have getting out of here would be remaining unnoticed.
9. The conversation of this group lacked logical succession.
   The conversation was filled with non sequiturs.
10. My concern about most of these people did not weigh too heavily because they were out of their element.
    I wasn't too concerned about most of these people, because they really didn't belong here.

The Stand-in-fors (Pronouns)

The Spivak pronouns were developed by mathematician Michael Spivak for use in his own writing. They can be used in a generic setting where the gender of the person referred to is unknown, such as "the reader." They can also be used to describe a specific individual who has chosen not to identify emself with the traditional masculine (male) or feminine (female) gender.* The Spivak pronouns are: e—subject; em—object; eir—possessive (adjective); eirs—possessive (noun); emself—reflexive.

—Amanita.net

Recently, in going over a series of student assignments, I realized that the most egregious error in the writing was improper pronoun use (give the authors jail time!). Soon after, in reviewing a story I myself had written, I saw that *I* had also allowed the fuzzy (poorly defined) pronoun to stand in for a more exact noun. Then I started noting how, in conversation, I did the same thing. My own mistakes on the first draft and in natural speech lead me to caution that what we do by instinct isn't necessarily what we should do when we write. In writing, every word counts, though we'll hardly ever be able to reflect on the placement and implication of every intonation in a piece. If we did, we'd never get any writing out the door; we'd drive ourselves crazy. (So let's not be utterly perfectionistic.) On the other hand, in creating writing headed for print, we need to be conscious of the words to a much greater extent than when we're simply spouting off extempore.**

"Natural" isn't what we're looking for. We're seeking out a selective naturalism, a faux naturalism, a naturalism that appears natural, but is carefully picked out and worked over.

The problem in pronoun use isn't always that the reader won't understand by implication what the antecedent is, but that figuring out who or what is meant by an "it" or a "she" isn't the reader's job. I can't say this often enough, in fact: Figuring out the meaning of the words is not the reader's job. The *writer's* job is to set down the words as they are meant to be read. Passages with pronouns often call for deduction when the writer isn't clear. So, as writers, we must place our full attention on using the pronoun properly, at least until very careful use becomes second nature.

The basic rule regarding the antecedent for a pronoun is simple. The last proper or common noun (or certain type of pronoun, such as "all" or "each"—which don't themselves require antecedents) before the pronoun in question is the referent (the antecedent) to which the pronoun refers.

The reason that implementation can seem so difficult is that the writer is simply asleep at the switch. Wake up to pronoun use. Then all will be well.

> ❖ *Confusing/fuzzy*: Dave dined with his older brother and his wife, Sue.
>
> ❖ *Clear:* Dave dined with his older brother and Gerald's wife, Sue.

We might suspect in regard to the first sentence that Dave didn't bring his own wife to the dinner, since then the writer might have said, "Dave and his wife dined with Gerald, Dave's older brother." However, we can't be one hundred percent certain of the meaning. Even if the writer goes on to explain that the brother had been married to Sue for thirty years, the reader is still first forced into a period of uncertainly. Let's not be the ones to do that to the reader who has been so decent as to have picked up our material. (God bless all readers, everywhere.)

> ❖ *Confusing/fuzzy:* A jumble of unmarked crates randomly placed around the ship floor creaked in time

to the swing of a single, hanging light bulb. It barely illuminated this part of the hold.

❖ *Clear:* A jumble of unmarked crates randomly placed around the ship floor creaked in time to the swing of a single, hanging light bulb that barely illuminated this part of the hold.

❖ *Clear:* A jumble of unmarked crates randomly placed around the ship floor creaked in time to the swing of a single, hanging light bulb. The bulb barely illuminated this part of the hold.

Although we might hate to repeat the word "bulb," sometimes a repeat is preferable to a fuzzy pronoun. Granted, we might know what the "it" refers to, but the antecedent is still, logistically, unclear—even if legalistically sound. Logistics count. If we want to be admirable writing stylists, we will shrink from allowing a fuzzy pronoun of this nature. Heavens forefend. Give us a repeat any day over a fuzzy (ugh) pronoun. (Ptui.)

❖ *Confusing/fuzzy:* Despite the fact that she had been a ticket agent for twenty-three years, the airline didn't hire Alice.

❖ *Clear:* Despite the fact that Alice had been a ticket agent for twenty-three years, the airline didn't hire her.

Though we do sometimes place the pronoun *before* the antecedent, that can be confusing. Also, in this case, we might even think for a millisecond or two that the "she" is intended to refer to "airline." (Don't blame *me* for how the brain works.) If we want to write cleanly and clearly, our antecedents must be identifiable ninety-five percent of the time.

Here's a different kind of example of a missing antecedent:

> ❖ *No antecedent:* Bill was admitted to the hospital. Later that day Jim went to visit. They talked about the accident.
>
> ❖ *Correct use:* Bill was admitted to the hospital. Later that day Jim went to visit. The two men talked about the accident, then they decided what to tell Bill's wife.

Again, even though the reader knows very well who you're talking about (about whom), the example above is missing an actual, single noun antecedent for the "they." You must give an explicit antecedent.

> ❖ *No antecedent:* Eleanor's desk was a real oak beauty. She truly loved it.
>
> ❖ *Correct use:* Eleanor's desk was a real oak beauty, and Eleanor truly loved it.

A possessive is not a valid antecedent because a possessive is an adjective. An antecedent must be an actual noun or pronoun. This is a major goof that is often made, and I have seen it made even in a grammar class instructional. Don't let us make that mistake ourselves.

> ❖ *No antecedents:* Her mom was staying with her grandmother for a few days. She wrestled with whether or not to go, but finally decided to be with her mom, since she knew her dad wouldn't come to help. Although they didn't get along, she decided she owed her mother this much.
>
> ❖ *Correct use:* Pepper's mom was staying with her own mother for a few days, and Pepper wrestled with whether or not to go and stay there, too. Then she

> finally decided to be with her mom, since Pepper knew
> her dad wouldn't help out. Although Pepper and her
> mother didn't get along, Pepper decided she owed her
> mother this much.

Yes, we have to use Pepper's name five times in a short
paragraph, but that's correct and the sentences read pretty well,
despite the necessary repeats. In fact, the second version seems more
polished than the first, which is the case.

> ❖ *Incorrect pronoun use:* On a very cold winter day,
>   Jennie, a chocolate Lab, failed to return home in the
>   afternoon as expected. Hours later, her worried owner,
>   Obrah, and her dad went out in the car to look for her.
>   When found in an old barn, she was protecting a naked
>   baby girl by wrapping herself around her and licking
>   her vigorously.
>
> ❖ *Corrected:* On a very cold winter day, Jennie, a
>   chocolate Lab, failed to return home in the afternoon
>   as expected. Hours later, her worried owner, Obrah,
>   and Obrah's dad went out in the car to look for the dog.
>   When found in an old barn, Jennie was protecting a
>   naked baby girl by wrapping herself around the child
>   and licking her vigorously.

With three females in the paragraph, we need to be very exacting
with our antecedents, even though the reader might suspect what's
going on, anyway. You might note that the "herself" antecedent is
succeeded by another antecedent, but sometimes the author has to
do what the author has to do.

Gender Isn't the Issue

Let's suppose we know that one person under our (written)
discussion is a woman and the other a man. Wouldn't that confer an
automatic pass in terms of the antecedent rule? Can't we simply use
"she" whenever we reference Mary and "he" when we reference

Tom? No, not really. Although gender gives us a little bit of leeway so that we can cheat when doing so will make the writing less awkward, on the whole, we have to adhere to the antecedent rule in referencing humans, despite their gender.

> ❖ *Not quite:* Tom and Mary went to the meeting together, even though he was the representative of a competing firm.
>
> ❖ *Better:* Tom and Mary went to the meeting together, even though Tom was the representative of a competing firm.

Why must we do that? Let's just say we make this clear for the one person in ten thousand who will imagine that the "he" refers to Mary, whom the reader believes might be a man. Now in this sentence, the gender distinction can pretty much be said to be explicit, according to the typical set of names doled out in regard to "sex" in our society, but suppose the names blurred the distinction:

> ❖ *Not quite:* Tom and Miki went to the meeting together, even though he was from a competing firm.

Now that sentence might tend to be confusing because "Miki" could be either a man's name or a woman's, so we might simply correct for that ambiguity in this instance and say:

> ❖ *Better:* Tom and Miki went to the meeting together, even though Tom was from a competing firm.

But should the writer pick and choose where to distinguish between names in terms of gender nuance? He shouldn't. That's the purpose of a general rule. And the general rule doesn't distinguish between the genders. The rule is that the antecedent is the proper or common noun (or indefinite pronoun) just prior to the pronoun being decided on. So we must follow the antecedent as we would were the gender distinction not present. And that generalization will apply in ninety-nine percent of our writing. However, with language, almost nothing is that cut and dried, and sometimes another element will take precedence. I can promise you this much: We will be writing along swimmingly and come upon an instance in which following this rule will produce an awkward sentence, where clarification of gender is not really the issue. In such a case, we can throw caution to the wind; I say ignore the guideline and fudge the explicit antecedent.

Renew the Antecedent

No one says how long the antecedent will "last," and all I can tell you here is that the word doesn't echo on in the reader's mind forever. The "she," "she," "she" use might be fine for the writer, who has an image of Mary (or Miki) in her head, but the *reader* who has paused to (God forbid) run outside for a cigarette or to answer the phone may have forgotten Mary's name—two pages back—entirely. Let's continue to cater to the readers' frailties, poor dears, and reassert the antecedent every once in a while.

"How often do I need to do that?" asks the writer trying to achieve an admirable style. Well… The answer really depends on the author's ear, but we need to repeat the antecedent name or item name not infrequently. Again, the reader doesn't place the same importance on our words, or on our subject, that we do. His mind may well have wandered, even while he was sitting there. One thing we don't want as authors is for the reader to have to retrace his steps, to go back and skim to find out who "she" is. Simply tell the reader the antecedent with a fair amount of regularity.

The comment writers often make about this is, "But I didn't want to keep writing 'Jim,' 'Jim,' 'Jim.' " I understand. Really I do. But if any words in our writing are silent, they are the names of the subjects of the article or memo, or the character in fiction. They simply are.

The reassertion of the antecedent at the proper spot will honestly not jar. Yes, sometimes we might want to vary the location in which we place the name—not always giving the name again at the opening of every paragraph or always at a sentence start—but the repetition of the name itself will inform and not detract. So don't be afraid to use the name.

In fact, one warning in regard to names and the attempt to avoid repetition: Don't confuse the reader by using more than one name for the person or character. For instance, you don't want to refer to Bill Martin as "Bill" sometimes and as "Martin" at other times. Readers will simply wonder who you're talking about and, again, have to skim the preceding pages—not a task readers should be obliged to take upon themselves.

On the other hand, from time to time, you might call Bill "the woodcutter," if that's very clearly the man's trade. But be sure you have made that completely obvious before making the substitution.

One more point about renewing the antecedent. We must do that not only with regularity, but we must also renew the antecedent if more than a couple of sentences have lapsed since we used either the name or the pronoun. For instance:

> ❖ *Too long an interval:* She went into the other room. There, the photographs were laid out on the desk, marked as to date. The images had been taken with a camera brought back from a 1959 visit to Germany. The camera had a telephoto lens, and all these pictures had been snapped quite a distance from the subject. Aside from a set of about three dozen photos, her desk was otherwise clear.

The "her" is simply too far from even the "she," much less the person's actual name or other identification, to hold up. The topic has wandered afield from the person, and when we get back to any reminder of her, we need for the woman to be resubstantiated in full.

Antecedent/Pronoun Agreement

I see a lot of mistakes in this area in students' writing, and when I say "students," you have to understand that these are people who think of themselves as halfway to being writers already. Most of them probably do have somewhat better than average language abilities, but at the same time make an average set of grammatical and punctuation errors. If I see mistakes that my students pretty commonly make, I figure that the rest of us might make them as well.

The antecedent and the pronoun standing in for it must agree in number.

❖ *Incorrect:* The bank had razed the building when they moved their headquarters to a modern facility.

❖ *Correct:* The bank had razed the building when it moved its headquarters to a modern facility.

The bank is a singular entity, just as a company is. I know we tend to refer to a business as a "they," because we're thinking of the people working there, or the members of the board of directors who make the decisions for the impersonal corporation, but the company as such is an "it," a singular. While some grammarians say that when the collective noun acts or is regarded as multiple individuals it's plural, I'd just as soon see a clearer distinction made. A bank or a corporation is a singular legal entity.

This is what one grammar site takes as a correct usage: "The selection committee vote for their favorite candidates."

Well, the author here does have a point, though the sentence certainly sounds awkward as heck. Obviously incorrect is: "The selection committee *votes* for their favorite candidates."

However, we adjust for other little gaps in language, so why not here: "The selection committee members vote for their favorite candidates."

With a compound noun, we use a plural pronoun.

❖ *Correct:* Jack and Jane went to their weekly church meeting. But sometimes Jack and Jane do different things.

❖ *Correct:* Jack and Jane each made an appointment to go to each of their dentists in town.

Do I hear a question from the back of the room? Yes! (I have great metaphorical hearing.) The man in the black leather jacket wants to know why we couldn't use the plural pronoun when we said: "Bill was admitted to the hospital. Later that day Jim went to visit. They talked about the accident." Or, why can we use a plural pronoun now when we speak of Jack and Jane?

Good question, fella. The reason is that in the first instance, we don't have an antecedent and don't have a compound subject. In the second instance, we have a compound subject (the antecedent), which takes a plural pronoun. If that's not clear, ask me again after class (heh heh).

Be sure to use plural nouns/pronouns for things possessed if the subjects (or sometimes objects) are plural:

> ❖ *Correct:* Give Jim and Lester their pay slips before they leave for the evening.
>
> ❖ *Correct:* Jim and Lester, who are my colleagues, have good hearts.
> Jim and Lester don't share a paycheck or a heart.

Conversely with the "or" or "nor," the antecedent is taken as the noun (or pronoun) *nearest* the pronoun use being defined.

> ❖ *Incorrect:* Either the twins or Jennifer will go to their gym today. I can't drive both places.
>
> ❖ *Correct:* Either the twins or Jennifer will go to her gym today. I can't drive both places.

Of course, this sounds awkward, so I would personally change this to read:

❖ *Correct:* Either the twins or Jennifer will go to the gym today. I can't drive to both gyms.

❖ *Incorrect:* Everyone has their gear on and are ready to go.

❖ *Correct:* Everyone has their gear on and is ready to go.

❖ *Correct:* Everyone has his or her gear on and is ready to go.

❖ *Correct:* All the members have their gear on and are ready to go.

This is a stumper for anyone who writes in our contemporary society. How do we deal with such a pronoun ("everyone") in terms of gender? My best advice is that you choose an alternative that is maximally correct. In this book, you will notice that I use either the male or female pronoun more or less at random when a singular pronoun is required. In other writing of mine, I will usually change the singular antecedent to a plural.

Everyone, anyone, either, neither, much, one, no one, nobody, someone, somebody, something, nothing, everybody, and *anybody* are indefinite pronouns and are always taken as being singular. Plural pronouns include *both, many, several, few.*

Some pronouns are either singular or plural, depending on how they are used: *all, some, none, most.*

❖ *Correct:* All of them went to their lawyers' offices after being released on bond.

❖ *Correct:* All of it went into the folder where it belonged.

❖ *Correct:* The boys went to college. All returned to their high school later to thank the teachers.

> ❖ *Correct:* I put some of the trash back in its bin. (*Some as a singular.*)
>
> ❖ *Correct:* I went through the trash to find my keys, then I put the trash back in its bin.
>
> ❖ *Correct:* I put some of the statements into their proper envelopes before leaving. (*Some as a plural.*)
>
> ❖ *Correct:* The statements had been made up earlier, and I put some into their envelopes.
>
> ❖ *Correct:* None of the boys went to their homes after school.
>
> ❖ *Correct:* None of the money was returned to its owner.

As we see here, the determining factor can be the object of the prepositional phrase following the pronoun and describing it—or the determination of singular or plural can be made based on a factor presented prior to the use of the pronoun. But this variability only applies to pronouns that can be singular or plural. We can't say: "Either of them are…" We must say "Either of them is…" because "either" is a singular pronoun.

Reflecting Back On

I wasn't thinking about reflexives until I noticed students making mistakes in their use of this pronoun form. The misuse of a reflexive is a faux pas that causes everyone to gasp in horror. Not out loud, of course. But we don't want to appear ignorant while trying to speak—or write—carefully.

The basic rule for the reflexive (the pronouns *myself, yourself, himself, herself, itself, ourselves, yourselves,* and *themselves*) is that the word must have an antecedent to reflect back on. Without an antecedent, we cannot use a reflexive.

> ❖ *Incorrect:* George, Jim, and myself went to the store.

> ❖ *Correct:* George, Jim, and I went to the store, where I bought a turkey sandwich for myself.

The first sentence is incorrect because we have no "I" for the "myself" to reflect back on.

> ❖ *Incorrect:* George and Jim bought sandwiches for theirselves, too.
>
> ❖ *Correct:* George and Jim bought sandwiches for themselves, too.

The English language does not have such words as "heself," "hisself," "sheself," or "theirselves."

Even though a reflexive may seemingly be used correctly, in correct case and with the antecedent in the sentence, the use may still be incorrect.

> ❖ Incorrect: I expect they will be handing out subpoenas to everyone, including myself.
>
> ❖ Correct: I expect they will be handing out subpoenas to everyone, including me.

Here, the proper antecedent is no longer in force by the time we get to the "myself." We've had intervening antecedents. For a reflexive to be used here, "they" will have to hand out subpoenas to "themselves."

The intensive is similar to the reflexive—virtually identical, to be honest—but its function is to reemphasize a noun or pronoun.

Although, unlike with the reflexive, we can use an intensive in the subject position, even in subject case we do not use a subject case intensive, as these do not exist.

> ❖ *Wrong:* James heself went to Africa with Jane. *(Subject case doesn't exist.)*
>
> ❖ *Correct:* James, himself, went to Africa with Jane.
>
> ❖ *Correct:* She herself finished the project.

We can either use the comma pair around the intensive or not.

Of course, the noun or pronoun that is the antecedent for the intensive doesn't have to be in subject case:

> ❖ *Correct:* He gave Jane herself the letter.

Not Nebulous

I've complained elsewhere or will complain, depending on the order in which the pieces are published and in which you read them, about the use of the "it was" phrase. Here I'm going to gripe solely about a common use of "it," that is, the use of "it" without a concrete antecedent.

> ❖ *Vague:* We had no money for lunch that day, and it made me feel pretty depressed.
>
> ❖ *Concrete:* We had no money for lunch that day, and not being able to eat made me feel depressed.
>
> ❖ *Concrete:* We had no money for lunch that day, and being so broke made me feel depressed.

When the writer tries to use a concept as an antecedent rather than a concrete noun, the reader must guess the exact meaning of the pronoun. Let me state again what I said above (and what I've said elsewhere)—the reader's job is not to guess the meaning of the sentence. The writer's job is to tell us what she means.

Case in Point

I've mentioned "case" a few times, so let's just review the concept. Some languages change the form of nouns depending on their use in speech. The Romans did this when they spoke Latin, and the Germans take this approach today, though by changing the article rather than the noun per se. We, too, have a remnant of such a linguistic style in the changes we make in our English pronouns, depending on their use as subject, object, or possessive. Nouns as well as pronouns show possessive case. I (subject) asked him (object) to give them (object) to me (object), but he (subject) objected (verb—a little joke here, dear reader), saying they (subject) were his (possessive) children, not mine (possessive) and had lives of their (possessive) own. My (possessive) answer was that they (subject) were my (possessive) sister's kids.

The use of the wrong pronoun case isn't a writing error made as frequently as one might fear, but such a mistake is definitely made and doesn't give a good impression of the writer's level of education or even intelligence. Therefore, we want to be careful to use the correct case. Using the correct case takes an analysis of the sentence, and that's where many English speakers and writers fall down.

People can't always tell subject from object. The subject is the topic of the sentence or the initiator of some action, as in "I (subject) asked..." The object is the recipient of the action "I asked him (object)..." or the recipient of the movement of a preposition, as in "to me."

Writers often also fail to use possessive case with a gerund. Here are some examples of possessives used with gerunds: His (possessive) writing (gerund) improved by leaps and bounds when he finally was able to concentrate. But today Molly's (possessive) singing (gerund) in the shower was his (possessive) undoing (gerund).

Sometimes case is missed in an elliptical sentence. I heard one on a television news program the other day:

> ❖ *Incorrect*: Even though Kobayashi's competitors were larger, they ate less than him.

> ❖ *Correct:* Even though Kobayashi's competitors were larger, they ate less than he.

The "than he" really stands for "they ate less than he did."

Who *vs.* Whom

One pronoun that gives some writers a bit of a run for their money in terms of case is "who" and its permutations. "Who" is subject case and "whom" is object case. The problem here, however, is that the use of the object case doesn't always appear natural. "Whom" often sounds stiff: "Give the money to the members to whom money is important."

This is one grammatical rule I am sometimes willing to bend in my own work. If the writing is formal—an article to appear in an industry publication, a memo, a proposal, a letter—I will use the "whom" where it is required by the rule. In fiction, though, when writing about characters who would definitely not be able to tell whom from who themselves and for readers who don't care, I will use "who" at times even when the "whom" is grammatical.

In fiction we don't usually want to sound overly formal for some types of stories. Thus, my advice is to be pragmatic. We should know the rule and apply it as we feel the situation demands. In fiction in particular, we don't want our language use to become a distracting focus of reader's thoughts. Let's be a little flexible.

The other "who" issue is the difference between "whose" and "who's." "Whose" is the possessive, as in "Whose singing was that?" (Nice to see that we can use the "whose" with a gerund, isn't it?) "Who's" is a contraction for "who is," as in "Joe is the one who's going to Idaho State on a football scholarship."

* You *can* use them, but I don't recommend it.

** I want to tell this story, so I will. (I'm the one writing the book.) I gave a student feedback on an assignment today and she said thanks, adding that she must have misunderstood the instruction. She didn't realize this was anything but an informal little essay. Or, in other words, she didn't understand that I would correct her writing. Hello! You're writing something and you put it out there and you don't expect what? You don't expect anyone to *notice* grammatical errors? Or you don't expect anyone to think badly of you because you've made those errors? Or you don't expect anyone to be so rude as to mention your errors?

I have to tell you, dear reader: This happens all the time. Something is wrong here. Please, in life, we have to do our best *all the time* at whatever we're doing. We *are* being judged. Whatever we're putting out *is* being noticed. Casual efforts are not good enough. We don't have to be perfect. We don't. Writers have to allow themselves both to experiment and to fail. But casual efforts? I don't think so.

Here's the Zen story on the topic of effort. A dying Zen master gets up from his death bed and dances around. His students who had been gathered by his side stand back in complete astonishment. The master lies down again, and as he takes his last breath, tells his students, "Now that's effort."

Okay, I got carried away, but let's forget being half hearted about our undertakings.

Exercise

Part I.

Correct the following:

A "skip tracer" is an investigator specializing in locating people that skip out on his or her debts. Frank Ahearn, whom can be reached by email and phone, is a skip tracer extraordinaire. He subcontracts to take on other investigators' hardest cases. But what he also does is help people to disappear. However, he doesn't take on someone sleazy. He investigates them hisself before helping them vanish. His clients are whistleblowers in fear of his life or women escaping her dangerous stalker. In one case, while looking for a subject, he realized the man was stalking her. At that point, Ahearn told her what to do.

Whether one can disappear successfully or not depends on money. You have to pay to disappear and, beyond that, he or she needs a certain amount to live on in their new life. If they work again at the same job, they are in a predictable situation, one in which you will be found.

Claim your free access to www.firstwriter.com: See p.263

Using misinformation, Ahearn and his partner take the person whom is being stalked's current information and she messes it up. By the time an investigator makes some calls trying to find the client, everything, including their Social Security number, has been altered.

Part II.
Correct the following:
1. I wanted to get my dog, Jack, to the vet so he could give it its shot.
2. All of the money were in my account.
3. That was her playing the guitar outside your window.
4. She asked who's singing that was.
5. Anne wanted to know whom was singing.
6. Mr. Frank's home is here. He's our coach.
7. None of the boys went to their classes on time.
8. I hope they give theirselves a break.
9. They will probably pay all of us, including myself.

Answers

Part I.
A "skip tracer" is an investigator specializing in locating people *who* skip out on *their* debts. Frank Ahearn, *who* can be reached by email and phone, is a skip tracer extraordinaire. He subcontracts to take on other investigators' hardest cases. But what he also does is help people to disappear. But *Ahearn* doesn't take on *anyone* sleazy. He investigates *clients* before helping them vanish. *Ahearn's* clients are whistleblowers in fear of *their lives* or women escaping *their* dangerous *stalkers*. In one case, while looking for a subject, *Ahearn* realized the *client* was stalking her (*that's a tricky one, and this pronoun use is a best bet solution*). At that point, Ahearn told *the female subject* what to do.

Whether one can disappear successfully or not depends on money. *The person who wants to disappear has* to pay *for help* and, beyond that, he needs a certain amount to live on in *his* new life. If *the person works* again at the same job, *he is* in a predictable situation, one in which *he* will be found. Using misinformation, Ahearn and his partner *mess up the current information of the person who* is being stalked. By the time an investigator makes some calls trying to find the *missing person*, everything, including *her* Social Security number, has been altered.

Part II.

1. I wanted to get my dog, Jack, to the vet so he could give it its shot.
    I wanted to get my dog, Jack, to the vet so the vet could give Jack his shot.
2. All of the money were in my account.
    All of the money was in my account.
3. That was her playing the guitar outside your window.
    That was she playing the guitar outside your window.
4. She asked who's singing that was.
    She asked whose singing that was.
5. Anne wanted to know whom was singing.
    Anne wanted to know who was singing.
6. Mr. Frank's home is here. He's our coach.
    Mr. Frank's home is here. Mr. Frank is our coach. (The "he" had no antecedent.)
7. None of the boys went to their classes on time.
    Correct.
8. I hope they give theirselves a break.
    I hope they give themselves a break.
9. They will probably pay all of us, including myself.
    They will probably pay all of us, including me.

There Was an 'It Was,' Wasn't There?

Many a tame sentence of description or exposition can be made lively and emphatic by substituting a transitive in the active voice for some such perfunctory expression as "there is" or "could be heard."
—Strunk and White's The Elements of Style

"It was the best of times, it was the worst of times..."
—Charles Dickens
opening *A Tale of Two Cities*, and referring to the period of the French Revolution.

The exhortation for the writer to avoid passive forms has rung out through the ages—or at least for a while. Many writers, however, don't know how that shows up or how the problem can be fixed. To start with, the simple static structure problem is as common as white bread. And because these forms are so ubiquitous, writers reproduce them without seeing them as empty, meaningless placeholders. Keep your wits about you as you write, and look for some of these.*

❖ *Static:* It was a staggering defeat.

❖ *Active:* The defeat at Waterloo, with its thirty-four thousand French casualties, staggered the nation.

You will find that when we switch from static to active, we often have to bring greater detail into the sentence. The tame or perfunctory or static forms such as "it was" and "there was" serve in place of solid fact, so that a determination to rid ourselves of these meaningless, rote phrases will force us to add interesting words and specificity. The need to add detail is a worthwhile benefit of writing in active voice, as expanding meaning in any type of written piece gives the reader more material of interest.

When I see this type of form (the *it was* or *there was* formation) and I'm tired of making suggestions to students as to how they can change from static writing to active, I often simply write "What's the subject?" or "Find the subject."

The main technique for moving from static writing to active voice is to find the subject and verb and construct the sentence around those. The reason I don't mention the verb all the time is that the verb may remain the same (a "to be" form).

❖ *Passive (static):* It was childish of her.

❖ *More dynamic:* She was childish.

❖ *Static:* It looked as if he was ill.

❖ *More dynamic:* He looked ill.

Bear in mind that with all these sentences starting with an "it," that the "it" doesn't serve its proper role as a pronoun in that the word stands in for nothing at all. The writer mainly uses the "it" out of laziness, instead of finding a concrete subject, or finding a concrete subject and pairing that noun or noun plus adjective (or pronoun) with a dynamic verb. The opportunity to replace a weak verb with a more powerful one can be another benefit of moving from stagnant to more active voice.

❖ *Stagnant:* It was childish of her.

❖ *More active:* She was childish.

❖ *Stronger:* She behaved childishly.

The *it was, it is, it's* forms pervade our literary world. And in some instances, this particular way of expressing ideas has become the gold standard of English language writing.

❖ *Standard:* It was raining.

❖ *Variant:* The skies opened up.

❖ *Variant:* The rain had been falling for some time now.

Using the two variants, though they are more forceful here, might create too great a focus on the rain. Perhaps the rain is a minor element and we don't want to emphasize it.

❖ *Standard:* It was raining.

❖ *Variant:* An aide to the secretary met Prime Minister Blair with an umbrella.

❖ *Standard:* It was March.

❖ *Variant:* The March meeting took place in San Diego.

Because we are so used to many commonplace expressions, and they seem so innocuous, we find nothing wrong with the standard format. Revising the standard use may seem a bit pretentious or too efforted, in fact. Certainly we don't want to go overly crazy in our attempts to assert the active voice. But on the other hand, once we bring the static/active distinction to mind, we might begin to find that the implementation even in "standard" situations may carry us from standard to a cut above in our writing style. Of course, the intention of the piece must always rule, and we don't want our writing to be too formal or elaborate if it (we have an antecedent here) doesn't need to be.

Sometimes a Gerund

A gerund is a noun formed by adding an "ing" to the verb. Not infrequently, writers will use an "it was" format in the place of creating and using a gerund as the sentence subject. Creating the gerund and thus having a "real" subject is a more dynamic way of writing than using the static "it is" sentence start.

❖ *Static:* It was best for us to go through the crowd rather than avoid it.

❖ *Active with gerund:* Going through the crowd rather than avoiding it seemed best.

❖ *Active with revision:* We decided the best route was through the crowd rather than around it.

When we choose the gerund form as the subject, the verb often is pushed toward the end of the structure (sentence two). However, this is a more forceful sentence approach than using the static opening (sentence one), even though the static format offers the verb close to the start. Obviously, using an active verb (sentence three) creates the most dynamic sentence.

There Was/There Were

Nearly identical with the *it was* format is the *there was* means of opening a sentence or a clause. Just as the *it was*, *it's*, and *it is* without a proper antecedent for the *it* stand as placeholders for genuine nouns and verbs, so, too, are *there was*, *there's*, *there were*, and *there is* phrases used in the same way.

❖ *Static:* There were so many children in the orphanage that he couldn't care for them all without help.

❖ *Active:* The orphanage had so many children that he couldn't care for them all without help.

Often with these sentences, we don't need to insert any word, but we can use the words given and simply rearrange them. Our ability to reconstruct and eliminate the passive phrases shows that the words weren't needed in the first place.

❖ *Active with the same words:* So many children were in the orphanage that he couldn't care for them all without help.

❖ *Revised with a stronger verb:* So many children lived in the orphanage that he couldn't care for them all without help.

True Passive Voice

Another way the writer fails to assert active voice is by reversing the actor and acted upon, making the acted upon the subject of the sentence and inserting a passive verb form. This format is what is actually meant when we use the expression *passive voice.*

❖ *Passive:* The dog was taken for a walk.

❖ *Active:* Joe took the dog for a walk.

But bear in mind: Though such a form is passive and not the best way to write a sentence, this type of passive structure (sentence one) can be a better choice than the use of an insubstantial "there was" or "it was" phrase.

❖ *Static:* There was some information kept from John.

> ❖ *Improved but passive:* Some information was kept from John.
>
> ❖ *Active:* His parents kept some information from John.

The writer might have a reason to avoid the most active form of a sentence of this type. Perhaps he doesn't want to reveal who kept the information from John, or maybe we don't know at this point who deprived John of the information. Therefore, the improved but still passive form can be used. The most important factor when we choose which type of sentence to use—static, improved but passive, or active—is that we remain conscious of our options, and that we decide which to use on the basis of the goals we're trying to achieve in writing the sentence.

What the Dickens?

I quote Dickens at the top of this chapter with a sense of irony. Of course Dickens was not only the best of his day, but today's critics would still give much of his prose high marks. Certainly few sentences in English literary history are as well respected as the opening of *A Tale of Two Cities*:

> ❖ It was the best of times, it was the worst of times, it was the age of wisdom, it was the age of foolishness, it was the epoch of belief, it was the epoch of incredulity, it was the season of Light, it was the season of Darkness, it was the spring of hope,
>
> ❖ it was the winter of despair, we had everything before us, we had nothing before us, we were all going direct to Heaven, we were all going direct the other way—in short, the period was so far like the present period, that some of its noisiest authorities insisted on its being received, for good or for evil, in the superlative degree of comparison only.

The sentence is not one I'd care to go in and tinker with, as Dickens expresses so much wit and intelligence in these words. (Okay, a little tightening wouldn't be amiss, and I'd fix the punctuation.) However, he goes on:

> ❖ There were a king with a large jaw and a queen with a plain face, on the throne of England; there were a king with a large jaw and a queen with a fair face, on the throne of France. In both countries it was clearer than crystal to the lords of the State preserves of loaves and fishes, that things in general were settled for ever.

Enough with the passive voice, Charles. I simply must take out my red pencil.

> ❖ A king with a large jaw and a queen with a plain face sat on the throne of England; a king with a large jaw and a queen with a fair face sat on the throne of France. In each country the lords of the state preserves of loaves and fishes perceived more clearly even than crystal that the social order was settled for good.

Please note that once we start fiddling with the writing, we might as well go on and adjust every word at will. Do also note that the tendency to continue shaping the words doesn't just arise from a love of messing around with someone else's writing. Because we perform a delicate balancing act with words in a sentence, once we alter one piece, other elements must often be refashioned as a direct consequence.

Dickens really was a marvelous writer, but the style of the times in which he wrote favored the passive. Thus, Dickens was, himself, subject to the use of passive forms. In our era, we opt for active voice and a lean writing style. We invoke new strategies of word use that allow us to serve the mental tendencies of the readers of our own day. (That's the stuff I'm teaching you in this book, guys. *NB!*)

That some readers in the 21st century don't like to wade through the prose of certain vaunted authors of the past, in my opinion, doesn't mean that today's readers are lazy, stupid, or not intellectual. Their preference simply may have been formed by the reading and writing ideals of our own time. And, perhaps prejudicially, I myself feel that our leaner, tighter writing approach does have a greater merit than the florid or passive styles of the past.

Get Personal

The problem with some of the passive sentences above, such as "It was childish of her" or "It was best for us to go through the crowd" is not just that they are static, but that they are impersonal. In addition to these statements having no real subject, we can also say that no person takes responsibility for the action, thought, or feeling expressed. That is, the writer ought to inject into the sentence the person or persons who is/are the originator of the action or mood.

Writing that stands without a person as the subject when a human would ordinarily be in the subject place gives the reader the feeling that the sentence is vague and tentative, indirect, and unreliable. I often sense that the person producing such writing doesn't himself want to be accountable for the work he creates. He doesn't want to be visible.

❖ *Impersonal and passive:* The work being produced lacked some ingredient.

❖ *Active:* His work lacked some essential ingredient.

❖ *Impersonal and passive:* The homework was done for school.

❖ *Active:* He completed his school homework Friday night.

❖ *Impersonal and static:* It felt like entering a private estate, not the public library.

❖ *Active:* I felt as if I were entering a private estate, not the public library.

When we write sentences that express an action or a sensation obviously involving a human hand or emotional reaction, we should properly attribute that action or feeling (or thought) to a human or humans. Otherwise, the reader winds up in an eerie, unpeopled ghost world of words, words, words, with not a creature similar in kind to himself in sight. The homework completes itself and houses are built on their own accord.

In other instances, also less than ideal, the human(s) might be in the sentence but not in his/her/their rightful place.

❖ *Impersonal and static:* It seemed that he was in a dream state.

❖ *Active:* He seemed to be in a dream state.

Sometimes the writer ascribes part of the action or thought to human agency, but leaves out other aspects that should be attributed.

❖ *Impersonal and static:* I find that a host of ideas come to mind while biking. I carry a handheld device for whenever spectacularly awesome ideas surface.

❖ *Active and personal:* I find that a host of ideas come to my mind while I'm biking. I carry a handheld device and record whenever I entertain spectacularly awesome ideas.

Of course, the writing here could be improved and be even more succinct and active.

Lack of attribution often results in a dangling/misplaced modifier.

❖ *Dangling modifier:* Upon entering the room, two things were immediately apparent—a dead body lay on the floor and the window was open.

❖ *Appropriate modifier:* Upon entering the room, she immediately noticed two things—a dead body on the floor and an open window.

❖ *Dangling and misplaced modifiers:* Becoming a freelance commercial artist will allow my schedule to be flexible to accompany my husband in his travels.

❖ *Appropriate modifiers:* My becoming a freelance commercial artist will allow my schedule to be flexible so that I can accompany my husband on his travels.

The expressions "dangling modifier" and "misplaced modifier" are most often used interchangeably, although sometimes the initial misplaced modifier, specifically, is called "dangling."

Whenever and as often as possible, without straining the limits or respectability of the English language, write in the active voice. Using the active voice in one sentence seems like such a small improvement, but converting an entire essay or manuscript from weak, passive sentences to the active voice causes the reader to experience the warmth and passion of your message and, as an extra bonus, tends to be less wordy. To convert a passive sentence to an active one, you first must recognize passive writing. Look for two passive signals: (1) form of the verb "be" such as "is," "are," "was," or "were" and (2) the word "by."

These signals often appear in sentences where the verb precedes the subject, analogous to placing the proverbial cart before the confused horse. To convert such a sentence to the active voice, ask yourself what or who is performing action and allow that subject to precede the verb.

Hats off to Professor Larkins

Lord, that man sure do write well

"Consider the following passive sentence: 'All the students in his graduate tax class were put soundly to sleep by Dr. Larkins.' The subject or 'horse' (Dr. Larkins) comes after the verb or 'cart' (put). Conveying the same message in stronger terms requires only that one walk the horse around to its rightful place before the cart: 'Dr. Larkins put all the students in his graduate tax class soundly to sleep.' In addition to the increased strength, the active form requires two fewer words.

~ Ernest R. Larkins

*Kathleen Dalton-Woodbury, who organizes online writing groups at Orson Scott Card's website, Hatrack River, calls such writing "static."

Exercise

Part I.

Make the following more active, less passive or static.
1. There was no reason for him to harass me.
2. It was a bright spring day at last.
3. It felt as if an emotional bomb had been dropped.
4. It felt as if I had been tricked into doing something I hated.
5. I was especially captivated by the red evening gown.
6. Without a leader, our party never got off the ground.
7. A few days earlier, the preparation had begun for our party.
8. There is a curfew in place that must be obeyed.
9. The ice pack went on his head.
10. The stairs led him down to the basement.

Part II.

Answer the following:
1. What is the difference between active voice and passive?
2. Should we ever use passive voice?
3. Can we say "It was raining"?
4. What are the tip-offs that passive voice has been used?

5. What's a misplaced modifier?
6. What's a dangling modifier?
7. What is the meaning of "static phrase"?
8. Which two static phrases are the most frequently used in writing?
9. What did Strunk and White call a sentence with static phrasing?
10. Should we ever write a sentence without a person?

Answers

Part I.

Your version may be good, but here are some possible changes:

1. There was no reason for him to harass me.
   He had no reason to harass me.
2. It was a bright spring day at last.
   At last we had a bright spring day.
3. It felt as if an emotional bomb had been dropped.
   Everyone seemed to feel as if an emotional bomb had been dropped.
4. It felt as if I had been tricked into doing something I hated.
   I felt as if I had been tricked into doing something I hated.
5. I was especially captivated by the red evening gown.
   The red evening gown captivated me.
6. Without a leader, our party never got off the ground.
   Without a leader, we never got off the ground in organizing our party.
7. A few days earlier, the preparation had begun.
   A few days earlier, we had begun the preparations.
8. There is a curfew in place that must be obeyed.
   We must abide by the curfew that's in place.
9. The ice pack went on his head.
   He put the ice pack on his head.
10. The stairs led him down to the basement.
    He took the stairs down to the basement.

Part II.

1. What is the difference between active voice and passive?
   In passive voice, the subject is acted on, rather than being

the actor, as in active voice.

2. Should we ever use passive voice?
   Yes, we may use passive voice, and even static phrasing, if those are the best writing choices for the situation. However, an active writing style, overall, is preferable.

3. Can we say "It was raining"?
   We probably will use that type of construction from time to time, although we might want to consider variations.

4. What are the tip-offs that passive voice has been used?
   The use of a form of the word "be" and the use of the word "by."

5. What's a misplaced modifier?
   A modifier that doesn't properly attach to the noun or pronoun it's intended to modify. The noun or pronoun may not even be in the sentence, in fact.

6. What's a dangling modifier?
   This is another phrase describing a misplaced modifier.

7. What is the meaning of "static phrase"?
   A static phrase is one that doesn't advance the meaning of the sentence, but serves simply as a sort of "placeholder."

8. Which two static phrases are the most frequently used in writing?
   "There is" and "it is" are two of the most widely used static phrases.

9. What did Strunk and White call a sentence with static phrasing?
   Tame.

10. Should we ever write a sentence without a person?
    Of course. That was a trick question. "The dog trotted along briskly."
    "The new red bicycle stood by the door." However, we do want to try for well-defined sentence subjects, where possible.

Parallel Forms

The likeness of form enables the reader to recognize
more readily the likeness of content and function.
—Strunk and White's *The Elements of Style*

Something in (wo)man loves careful organization and a well-balanced architecture of the written word. Our linear minds have evolved to allow a basically simple organism (us) a means of dealing with a super-complex universe out there. We seek order lest we fall into the survival-threatening chaos that underlies a polydimensional reality we're entirely incapable of tracking....

Okay, never mind all that: Make your writing orderly by using parallel constructions.

> ❖ *Not parallel:* Bob would look back with an expression on his face like a child who was breaking a rule.
>
> ❖ *Parallel:* Bob would look back with an expression on his face like that of a child who was breaking a rule.

Here, "expression" is the word being compared through the use of the preposition "like." (Yeah, *like* serves here as a preposition—surprising, isn't it?) To have a comparison, however, we must provide equivalent terms for the reader to weigh. In the first version of the sentence, we don't have a reasonable comparison. Should we compare "expression" and "child"? I don't think so. So we have to find the proper counterbalance to Bob's "expression." We need a parallel, and we can create one here with the "that of" phrase, which points back to the word "expression." Okay, that wasn't so hard. The only problem was knowing we needed the corresponding element for a comparison. Now we know.

> ❖ *Not parallel:* The kids climbed all over him like their new pet.
>
> ❖ *Parallel:* The kids climbed all over him as if he were their new pet.
>
> ❖ *Parallel:* The kids climbed all over him as they would a new pet.

This is similar to the first example, but in this case the "like" doesn't work in the new structure. Like is a preposition and doesn't go in front of a clause.

> ❖ *Not parallel:* She put on a dry shirt that was probably a size too small, but that was at least marginally more comfortable than the parts of her that were still wet and chilled.
>
> ❖ *Parallel:* She put on a dry shirt that was probably a size too small, but the top half of her was then at least marginally more comfortable than the bottom half, which remained wet and chilled.

Writers often think the reader is all knowing and can even read minds. Here, the second "that" in the nonparallel example is allowed to stand in for an unarticulated concept. As writers, we can at least spell out the words specifying what we mean.

> ❖ *Not parallel:* To find out about such work in your locale, check for signs in store windows, look on bulletin boards at grocery stores, in churches, and at schools.

❖ *Parallel:* To find out about such work in your locale, check for signs in store windows and look on bulletin boards at grocery stores, in churches, and at schools.

What we have here is a list of two things to do, with the second task subdivided into three. We don't have a list of four things to do. This is a pretty significant type of error, as I often find mistaken groupings of items. I think this relates to a failure to mentally articulate to oneself what is being said. Can we develop minds that are better able to make distinctions? I have to say yes. We can look more carefully at what we're actually saying and not sweep words under the proverbial rug. I used to do that as a reporter. If someone said something, I would repeat his words in an article even though I might not have really understood. Then I woke up and said, "Hey, if I don't understand, why do I think the reader will?" I now don't repeat what I don't understand, and I think my writing is clear and readable. (I could be wrong.)

❖ *Not parallel:* The newsletter will appeal to the mature adult, both in and outside of childhood education.

❖ *Parallel:* The newsletter will appeal to the mature adult, both inside and outside of childhood education.

When we can have parallel forms such as "inside" and "outside," why would we not?

Logic can also require the reorganization of structures in a process that is somewhat similar to creating a parallel.

❖ *Not a logical flow:* His body broke down after it could no longer take the assault by man and germs and machines.

> ❖ *Logical flow:* His body broke down after it could no longer take the assault by germs and man and machines.

Here, the mind would go from germs to man to machine rather than from man to germs to machine, because our minds operate in a linear fashion. Germs would assault the patient first, then man would intervene with his "healing" modalities, then the machines would be attached. (True that we have a nonlinear aspect to us, but that part isn't the mind, and we generally write to the mind [as well as the emotions] so we *must* suit the mind.)

The writer's job is to create order out of chaos. That we sometimes seem to create chaos is also true (as in Alain Robbe Grillet's *Last Year in Marienbad*, to date myself), but this is to achieve a more emotional effect on the reader by making logic an impossible path. Does this sound Zen? Well, something like that. We use lack of reason to stop the mind and force the reader to find something new.

> ❖ *Not parallel:* The horrid gargoyles were still there, still flapping wings against the bright moon. Still painting the far wall with their terrifying shadows. And the beady eye was staring right down at him.
>
> ❖ *Parallel:* The horrid gargoyles were still there, still flapping wings against the bright moon. Still painting the far wall with their terrifying shadows. And the beady eye stared right down at him.

We don't want to use the participles "flapping" and "painting" and then use the progressive verb "staring" as if we were introducing a sort of parallel, which we really can't claim.

> ❖ *Not well-structured:* She listened to their quiet talk, the flat monosyllables that rose from the nightmare of what had occurred. The waves of light and the

changing rhythm of voices, music, laughter, and applause from the television in the corner registered on her eyes and ears, but none of it meant anything to her.

❖ *Improved:* She listened to their quiet talk, the flat monosyllables that rose from the nightmare of what had occurred. The changing rhythm of voices, music, laughter, and applause from the television in the corner registered on her ears, while her eyes took in the waves of light radiating off the TV screen. But none of all this meant anything to her.

When discussing one aspect of anything, we ought to stick with that aspect until we switch to the next aspect. At that point, we don't go back to the first aspect, unless drawing a comparison. So, here, the writer needs to finish discussing the varieties of what the point of view person is hearing before going on to visual effects. The transition should be clear.

❖ *Not parallel:* For several moments there was stunned silence amid the acrid smell of the gunpowder.

❖ *Parallel:* For several moments, the crowd reacted with stunned silence. He stood quietly, while breathing in the acrid smell of gunpowder.
(The auditory sense has to be decoupled from the sense of smell. They can both be expressed, but distinctly.)

❖ *Not parallel:* We included the following stops on our trip:
• Paris,
• Boxing in London,
• Seeing the castle in Edinburgh
• Then going to Wales.

❖ *Parallel:* We included the following stops on our trip:
• Paris,

> • London (we saw some boxing),
> • Edinburgh (a city dominated by its castle), and
> • Cardiff (we also visited the incredible Snowdonia National Park).

Always make bulleted points or lists of any type parallel in structure.

> ❖ *An awkward parallel:* The dog started to growl and bare its teeth at me.
>
> ❖ *Improved:* The dog started to growl and bared its teeth at me.

What is meant here? Did the dog start to growl and start to bare its teeth? Or did it start to growl and then, separately, bared its teeth? We want to always make the verbs (or any listings) parallel if they are parallel and distinct if they are distinct, and we do that by first understanding what we mean to express. I believe this is a sequenced statement. The dog started to growl and then it bared its teeth. So started and bared are the two parallel verbs, not growl and bare.*

> ❖ *Not parallel:* That night the gypsy came to the house at 8 p.m. She had a yellow scarf wrapped around her head, large shiny gold earrings, a long crooked nose, and her teeth were big and white.
>
> ❖ *Parallel:* That night the gypsy came to the house at 8 p.m. She had a yellow scarf wrapped around her head; large shiny gold earrings; a long crooked nose; and big white teeth. (*Semicolons may be used with long phrases.*)

I actually don't like this clumping together of description. We might be better off saying, "The gypsy came at 8 p.m., a yellow scarf wrapped around her head as if an accent to a pair of big gold earrings. Inside, her large white teeth flashed at us in the candlelight as she set up her cards on the coffee table. I noticed with fascination her long, crooked, witchy nose, the longest I had ever seen." I also don't like mixing the elements of dress with facial elements as if they were truly parallel, even though they are joined in that way in the above example by the word "had."

> ❖ *Not parallel:* She had inherited an eye for detail and her sense of logic from her mother.
>
> ❖ *Parallel:* She had inherited an eye for detail and a sense of logic from her mother.

Here, one small change creates the parallel. If we say "an" eye, we need to say "a" sense.

> ❖ *Not parallel:* She turned and gave Jerry the same old wicked smile she'd been doing since high school.
>
> ❖ *Parallel:* She turned and gave Jerry the same old wicked smile she'd been giving him since high school.

We don't really need the same verb for a parallel here, but we need an appropriate verb and "doing" isn't appropriate, so it ruins any parallel for the comparison. We could say "flashing at him" or some such and we'd have an appropriate parallel. The problem is really that we don't "do" smiles.

> ❖ *Not parallel:* Jean transformed herself from glamour to ordinary clothes, hair, and glasses.
>
> ❖ *Parallel*: Jean transformed herself from glamorous to ordinary by changing her clothes, combing out her hair, and putting on her glasses.

Need I explain this one? The first sentence is simply a mess.

*Is a dog an "it"? Dogs and other animals do have gender. The rule for expressing this is that if we know the gender, we may use the gender-associated pronouns—if we choose—or we can say "it," unless the dog is one familiar to us: "I love my dog, Cindy, and find her a lot of fun. I hate the dog down the block because it's a nuisance."

Exercise

Correct the following:

1. Her troubled sleep gave way to an even more peculiar day.
2. She wanted the money because if she worked there, she might be more popular.
3. One of the books that I have enjoyed reading is *The Hobbit* and the trilogy that followed it.
4. Isolation is the heart killer. Instead, host a party and invite fifteen to twenty friends and acquaintances.
5. I could not disclose to any of them where I was from, the substance we will take, or my mission.
6. Bringing anyone this far downtown was not his usual tour for guests.
7. She thought running and to go to the movies would make for a pleasant birthday.
8. People were in Washington from Russia, Virginia, Sacramento, and France.
9. I wanted to study to write, photography, archeological digs, and forensic psychology this semester.
10. He had a face like a puppy, and she took to him at once.

Answers

1. Her troubled sleep gave way to an even more peculiar day.
   Her troubled sleep gave way to an even more troubled day.
2. She wanted the money because if she worked there, she might be more popular.
   She wanted the money, but also, if she worked there, she might be more popular.
3. One of the books that I have enjoyed reading is *The Hobbit*

and the trilogy that followed it.

One of the books that I've enjoyed reading is The Hobbit. *I've also enjoyed the trilogy that followed it.*

4. Isolation is the heart killer. Instead, host a party and invite fifteen to twenty friends and acquaintances.

   Isolation is the heart killer. Instead of remaining isolated, host a party and invite fifteen to twenty friends and acquaintances.

5. I could not disclose to any of them where I was from, the substance we will take, or my mission.

   I couldn't disclose any number of my secrets, such as where I was from or my mission here. I wasn't going to speak about my experiments, either.

6. Bringing anyone this far downtown was not his usual tour for guests.

   The downtown area wasn't part of his usual sightseeing tour for guests.

7. She thought running and to go to the movies would make for a pleasant birthday.

   She thought running and then going to the movies would make for a pleasant birthday.

8. People were in Washington from Russia, Virginia, Sacramento, and France.

   People were in Washington from countries such as Russia and France. They also came from states in the U.S., such as Virginia and California.

9. I wanted to study to write, photography, archeological digs, and forensic psychology this semester.

   This semester I wanted to study writing, photography, archeology, and forensic psychology.

10. He had a face like a puppy, and she took to him at once.

    He had a face like a puppy's, and she took to him at once.

PART II
Refine Your Language

Don't Repeat Words

A person who hears "echolalia" will automatically
say "echolalia" and thus produce echolalia.
—Rolf-Peter Wille

Not every person's ear can detect the grating sound a repeated word makes when someone's eyes hit upon the word's second use. All right, maybe the word itself doesn't make the sound, but something inside the head of the editor, the boss, or the instructor does—even if the not-so-sophisticated reader hears nothing but silence. In terms of style, my strongest advice is, "Don't repeat." And I wouldn't break that rule for anything less than an undefined "it" aching for clarification or, as will happen from time to time, a word that simply can't be replaced by any other phrase or expression and can't be avoided (grrrr).

Words that don't have many viable alternatives in a thesaurus include door, window (house parts are tough to replace), hand, eyes (body parts are killers), and words entirely specific to the type of material we may be producing. I sometimes write about longterm care, for instance, in which a "facility" can be a "residence" —but not when I need to say "resident" nearby. And "resident" is a hard one to replace, since we don't refer to people who live in nursing homes as "patients."

Trust me, you are going to stumble across the problem of repeats in your own writing sooner or later, if you haven't already. And you will need to deal with the issue, because language elements tossed into a sentence in close proximity to their twins detract from a pleasing manner of expression. Now I've tried to avoid using the word "word" and the word "repeat" too many times in the above, but since repeated words form the topic of this chapter, that goal is a mighty hard one to achieve. Still, as an inability to produce substitutes for a subject word is inevitable in such a case, readers will generally accept this type of repetition as a built-in necessity.

However, the rule holds, even here: Avoid repeating whenever possible.

In order to bypass repeats, for one thing—the hardest part— you have to notice that you've used the same word more than once. Repeats are wily little devils, and they frequently creep into a piece when a trusting writer has his back turned. If you don't believe me, try reading for the tricky gremlins and get rid of as many as you can discover until you're absolutely positive they're all gone.

Now, let the article loll about for a few days. Keep it locked up in the computer, if you like, with the screen saver pulled down covering it from interference. Next thing you know, when you call up the manuscript for a further review, you'll find that one or two repeats have snuck in again—those pests! Okay, this time you're really sure every last repeat has been vanquished. Give the piece to another writer or a reading friend to scan. Voila. That's when a devious repeat (or two) once more intrudes. (This way lies madness.)

Developing greater alertness to your repeats is a progression, a part of becoming, overall, more conscious of every aspect of the writing. Here's where that trained inner ear kicks in. Just as the editor and your instructor or boss have become attuned over the years to that horrible noise the repeat produces, so, too, can you develop the ability to listen to the sounds the words give off. Once each and every word resonates for you, then you will be better equipped to track down and eradicate the repeat imps.

But beware. Sometimes the repeats aren't whole worlds or even actual repeats at all. They can be simply parts of words, such as the "dis" in "disturbed" used near to "distinguished." Or a so-called repeat can be caused by words that clash—that rhyme, for instance, when rhyming is a distraction.

The trained ear can uncover all types of repeats, and this tracking them down like an audio detective is step one in your repeat eradication program. Step two is to fix them. The following are some examples of the thought process that occurs when the writer replaces the repeat with a substitute for the word—or restructures the sentence to avoid the duplication.

❖ *Repeat:* In today's busy times, a calendar reminder can also be used. When I was a youngster, I used to keep a list at my study desk that listed several of the dates I wanted to remember.

❖ *Varied:* In today's busy world, a calendar reminder can also be used. When I was a youngster, I kept a list at my study desk noting several of the dates I wanted to bear in mind.

Sometimes a word has two meanings, such as "used" in the example above. The different implication of the second instance doesn't make the repeat any less annoying to the ear. Here, as I went to edit the sentences and remove the repeats, I noticed that the clause "I used to keep" didn't need all those words, including the "used," (which was a repeat). Although I had removed the first "used," when I came to the second and found a more efficient means of stating the same idea, I returned the first to the original form.

After the words "list" and "listed," the final repeat in the example sentences was "reminder" and "remember." These words are not identical, obviously, but close enough for the author to change one. Yes, you say, but what about the words "reminder" and "mind"? Those "repeats" are far enough from one another to allow both to stand. However, if you can find a substitute for one, so much the better.

❖ *Repeat*: He tore the fuzzy toy into two. The rip tore through her. The little boy threw the pieces down, stood, then stomped on them.

❖ *Varied:* He tore the fuzzy toy in two. The rip sliced her heart. The little boy threw down the pieces, stood, then stomped on them.

Claim your free access to www.firstwriter.com: See p.263

Sometimes a revision may not improve every aspect of the sentence. "The rip tore through her" might be better phrasing than "The rip sliced her heart." However, we really can't allow the second "tore" to stand. So, for the moment at least, we have to make the substitution. Notice also that the "into two" constitutes a repeat with the "to" and the "two." We can make a small deletion to repair that one.

Lastly, the "through" and "threw" have to be fixed. Here, the same sounding words have different meanings, and they are spelled differently. That makes the repeat a bit less obvious to the eye. Yet those of us who want to employ in all respects an admirable style will eliminate the repeat, even if the redundancy is not one hundred percent noticeable.

> ❖ *Repeat:* An hour later, in my own house, I gratefully crawled into my own bed.
>
> ❖ *Varied:* An hour later, in my own house, I crawled gratefully into my bed.

Writers will frequently repeat words deliberately, in order to draw attention to the repeat, as a stylistic device. Generally, I don't feel that works as well as expanding the meaning with a variation. However, I can imagine a reason to use the above repeat, which would be to contrast the "own" bed from some other bed. If that's the case, then the repeat would be justified in order to produce the meaning.

Note that in the second version I repositioned the words "crawled" and "gratefully" to try to adjust the rhythm, which changed with the deletion of "my own." I don't know if the alteration helps. I'll see next time I read through the sentences. (Hmm, the two sentences are about the same in terms of cadence.)

> ❖ *Repeat:* An auxiliary volunteer gave us directions and we straggled through the halls, fresh uniforms in

plastic bags slung over our arms, tote bags filled with bright white shoes slung over our shoulders.

❖ *Varied:* A volunteer gave us directions and we straggled through the halls, fresh uniforms in plastic bags slung over our arms, totes filled with bright white shoes hung over our shoulders.

This example uses a repeat that isn't the same word, but simply the same idea. "Auxiliary" and "volunteer" give us the same meaning here, so we only need to say "volunteer" ("volunteer" is the word that will probably be more easily understood by the reader). The change to "totes" and elimination of the second "bags" also helps to fix the sentence. "Slung" doesn't have to be used twice, as "hung" will do for the second use. However, "slung" and "hung" are quite similar, and a different word and formation might be chosen. We could say "totes filled with bright white shoes drooped from our shoulders." Or, "and our shoulders bent under the weight of carryalls filled with bright white shoes."

In fact, often we have many choices of substitution, and even major surgery can be employed to rid ourselves of an offending repeat. This cannot be considered going too far to fulfill our writing duties. Certainly, rewriting constitutes an inescapable part of our job as writers. We shouldn't be too lazy to shuffle the words around as required. If we decide that the sentence is "good enough," because we don't want to make the effort to revise, we're deluding ourselves when we say we want to write effectively. We have to go as far as need be to make the writing work—not just as far as we're "willing" to go. Sometimes a single sentence requires multiple rewrites. That's the process.

❖ *Repeat:* The coach passed around a half-full box of donuts. My stomach, already queasy with fright, lurched at the smell of coffee and the sight of the gooey donuts.

❖ *Varied:* The coach passed around a half-full box of donuts. My stomach, already queasy with fright, lurched at the smell of coffee and the sight of the gooey pastries.

Sometimes the substitution of a single word is easy, and sometimes we search and search for the exact right word, which may not come to mind. That's why word processors have a built-in thesaurus. No shame is involved in looking up replacements for a word. Using a reference is a time-honored tradition and the reason the thesaurus sells so well. In fact, those who hope to do quite a bit of writing should have a paper thesaurus as well as an electronic one. Although perhaps the book won't offer more word choices most of the time, on the one occasion you're really, really stuck, the print edition might come in handy.

❖ *Repeat:* He got himself into a boring conversation, full of reminiscences of a life fully led before the war.

❖ *Varied:* He got himself into a boring conversation, chockablock with reminiscences of a life fully led before the war.

Sometimes we will find a little-used word as a substitution.

Here, "chockablock" is a nice alternative to employ in place of "full." But when going for exotic vocabulary, consider the sophistication level of the audience.

❖ *Repeat:* When he was a teenager, he rode the rodeo circuit in California, bull riding.

❖ *Varied:* When he was a teenager, he followed the rodeo circuit in California, making every effort to stay on the back of an angry bull for more than a second or two.

The first version is kind of a nice tongue twister, but not much good in terms of smooth reading. This one presents some challenges, though, as many instances of this type of editing will. After all, the word "rodeo" describes a pretty specific type of event. So does "bull riding." One or the other has to change, and "bull riding" wins as a term that can be presented in another fashion. The second sentence may not be better than the first in some ways, but the redundancies in sentence one are too ludicrous to let stand. On the other hand, the sentence "… he followed the rodeo circuit in California, bull riding" would certainly be viable.

Search for the Word

Another technique that writers frequently use to get rid of repeats is to do searches on words by way of the "find" function of the word processor. Sometimes we know we use a certain word way too often. For instance, a writer might be prone to having her characters grin, just as, often, my own characters raise their eyebrows.

When we know these things about our writing, we can search— replacing with the same term (watch the problem of capitalizations)— and get a count of how many times the word is used. Twenty grins in a manuscript is probably going overboard. In fact, we might say in such a case that the word "grin" is a signature of this particular author. So, should we consider signature phrasing or "typical" vocabulary of the author a stylistic weakness in a book or article? Yes, we have to, for the same reason that repeats are a stylistic flaw. Unique and quirky phrases or words simply draw too much attention to themselves and distract from the meaning of the writing. The overuse of a signature turn of phrase can even become downright annoying to the reader. We may not always be able to avoid this personality expression, but we can, and should, try.

Another condition under which we might need to do a search is when we go back through the piece for, groan, yet another draft. At this point, we might not notice every word exactly, but only those that seem to be giving us trouble. Thus we might replace a problem word with one we've used further above or further below the spot at which we're polishing. Sometimes we'll get an eerie sense that we have other instances of the replacement word nearby. That's when we can do a search to good effect and clear up that doubt for ourselves.

One other search that we might want to do if we're especially paranoid or just starting out will be on the several words that are quite commonly used by nearly every writer using the English language, such as "look," "just," "as" (more about that one, later), "that," "but," "seems," "felt," and "was."

How many instances of a certain word should we have in a manuscript, then? Of course, that depends. But the more unusual or significant the word, the fewer times we should employ it. Unless we're producing an explanation of Einstein's formulas, for instance, we likely don't want to insert the word "infinite" more than twice in a whole book or once in a short article or story. That's the type of word that strikes us and will be remembered when we encounter it again later in the text. Other words can be sprinkled in more liberally because they are more common and, therefore, more silent.

"Said"

I can't (won't?) tell you how many times I've argued for curtailing the common citation "said." Alleged to be a soundless word by its supporters, "said" will easily be heard by any reader with a somewhat trained ear—but only when the repetition is overdone or is close by the last citation.

> ❖ *Repeat citation:* "Rates are expected to rise in June," said the broker, who further said that those intending to invest in bonds should wait until later in the year. "Rising price/earnings ratios in a rising rate environment are not a good sign," Weaver said.
>
> ❖ *Varied citation:* "Rates are expected to rise in June," said the broker, who advised that those intending to invest in bonds should wait until later in the year. "Rising price/earnings ratios in a rising rate environment are not a good sign," Weaver noted.

"Said" is the mainstay of the journalist, certainly, but it's not the only word in town. Other reasonably respectable citations may be used. Of course, house style in journalism will take precedence over the individual voice of the reporter. Moreover, for some publications, quotes with repeats will have to remain unchanged. I say some, because, as a journalist, I routinely change the language within quotes so that they will read better—but I'm a trade journalist and don't report on current events where accurate quotes are essential.

❖ *Repeat citation:* "I won't be going on the stage tonight," said the cowboy. "You will if you know what's good for you," the banker said.

❖ *Varied citation:* "I won't be going on the stage tonight," warned the cowboy. "You will if you know what's good for you," the banker answered, biting off his words as if they were cigar tips.

An intransigent group of mystery writers are the primary culprits who stand up for the endlessly iterated "said." Why? Mystery author Elmore Leonard, who is quite a jokester, delivered a number of rules to those wanting to emulate his great success. Among them was the injunction to use no other citation than "said." True, Leonard does it, but that's his style. We don't want to be so foolish as to think we must follow a rule that, for us, will produce a less salutary effect.

Exercise

One reason why many writers set aside their work for a period of time is to hear the words anew when they read the piece again. After the writer takes a break from looking at the thing, he will find that the effect of repeated words and phrases becomes more evident. This is a great technique for those who have the time to wait. For those who don't, printing the work—or, vice versa, editing on the screen after a go-through with the printed version—will allow a change of perspective and the opportunity to detect more of the dreaded redundancy. That's the exercise, then, to use one or both of these techniques.

A second exercise, one many writers use even after a lifetime of experience, is to read the work out loud. Sometimes further repeats—and other infelicities—can be picked up this way.

Not Quite the Right Word

Twas brillig, and the slithy toves
Did gyre and gimble in the wabe:
All mimsy were the borogoves,
And the mome raths outgrabe.
> **—Lewis Carroll, "Jabberwocky"**

Not using the right word and lacking knowledge of a word's nuances are honestly tough problems to overcome. Mostly everything else in writing yields to generic logic or rules, but the use of the exact word to denote connotation comes from deep familiarity with the language. The person who doesn't come by the right word easily can only hope to improve through the study of vocabulary and by reading, reading, reading. Years of taking in words, especially the best of literature—that is, if the best appeals to us—will result in a treasure trove of words locked up in our nervous systems, which the right set of accompanying phrases will unlock. People who have a great background in devouring books often say that their own writing "just comes." That's because they have established the internal template.

Of course, don't be misled—no writing ever actually "just comes" and then can be trundled off to the publisher or sent in the mail to the magazine. Unless you are Stendhal, who wrote the amazing classic *The Charterhouse of Parma* in fifty-two days, or Yukio Mishima, who could write a novel by hand in a month, most of us have to at least edit what we've written to make the words come together properly in every way I discuss in this book.

Word choice is an overwhelmingly important part of that copyediting or polish process. Even if we get everything else right, the use of the wrong word, or a good word used wrongly (with the wrong preposition, say), will alert the agent, editor, teacher, or boss to the fact that we have difficulties writing in English.

Finding and using the right word is so very important that I'm going to share a few common glitches with you, as well as a few specific to the individuals who chose the wrong word. Unfortunately, most of those who do use the wrong word(s) make vastly different personal errors, so that no list could ever be complete or instructive enough to be worth compiling. That's why this is the hardest area of writing to correct. We don't know that we're misusing a word, and generally no one will take the time or be so impolite as to tell us. I'd take the time, if I had it, but I have no idea what you—YOU, individually (YOU)—are writing. Maybe some of the types of sentences you see below?

Simply Bad Choices

> ❖ *Poor choice:* Are you fat, floppy, and fed up?
>
> ❖ *Better choice:* Are you fat, flabby, and fed up?

Here, the writer can keep the alliteration and insert a word more proper to this use. I'm not sure what "floppy" means here. I have an impression, but the explicit meaning in this context eludes me. This is a case in which a writer merely thinks that because he knows how he's using the word, the reader will also know. And, in some sense, she probably will. Readers will bridge the gap because that's how the human mind tends to work. But should the reader stop to really consider the word, the error will be seen in glaring daylight. Suppose a mere five percent of readers stop and think. Or suppose the reader who stops and thinks is the editor. The word "floppy" will be tossed out.

> ❖ *Poor choice:* I've chosen doctors who were recently published in *New York Magazine* as being the best.

> ❖ *Better choice:* I've chosen doctors who were recently listed in *New York Magazine* as being the best.

The doctors weren't published, they were named or listed. Their names were published.

> ❖ *Bad choice:* Norwegian writer Knut Hamsun's novel, *Hunger*, put flesh on the mythological starving writer.
>
> ❖ *Better choice:* Norwegian writer Knut Hamsun's autobiographical novel, *Hunger*, made real the character of the allegorical starving writer.

You wouldn't want to use the word "flesh" in discussing a story of starvation, since starvation dissipates the flesh and the word calls attention to its own eerie implications.

> ❖ *Poor choice:* Not hailing from a rich family, Jack was accustomed to working hard every day.
>
> ❖ *Better choice:* Not from a rich family, Jack was accustomed to working hard every day.

"Hailing" is kind of a clumsy, old-fashioned word that we don't really use in this sense anymore (we still hail cabs).

> ❖ *Poor choice:* The flags were steadfastly mounted on top of the vehicles.
>
> ❖ *Better choice:* The flags were mounted securely on top of the vehicles.

To say the flags were steadfastly mounted would seem to mean that some stout-hearted worker mounted them.

> ❖ *Poor choice:* As many people around the world are now dying from obesity and fat-related issues as from starvation and malnutrition.
>
> ❖ *Better choice:* As many people around the world are now dying from obesity and fat-related health problems as from starvation and malnutrition.

We don't die from issues. This one isn't a matter of vocabulary, but of thinking about what we're writing. To be effective writers, we must be as logical as possible in our use of words.

> ❖ *Poor choice:* He designed many great buildings in his long and industrious career.
>
> ❖ *Better choice:* He designed many great buildings in his long and productive career.

He was industrious in doing his design work. His career was a productive one. Many words are used in very specific ways. We have to know the exact use of a word in choosing it. Here, these two words are very common ones, so the misuse of "industrious" is simply a glitch in the author's background. We all have those.

Okay, I just had an illumination. The writer meant "long and illustrious career," a common phrase. So this was a case of misunderstanding the spoken word. Who knew?

> ❖ *Poor choice:* I admit I contemplated chunking a rock or two at him.
>
> ❖ *Correct word use:* I admit I contemplated chucking a rock or two at him.

This is definitely a case of the writer having heard the word wrongly and then having gone on to hear the word wrongly many times over. One student, for instance, wasn't sure if she should use the word "input" or "imput." Of course, "imput" isn't a word at all. Her perception that two similar words existed was wrong.

> ❖ *Poor choice:* The odor permeated from the open fridge.
>
> ❖ *Better choice:* The odor emanated from the open fridge.

Here, the writer has taken a stab at the word, reaching and perhaps not quite finding the correct one in memory. That's one reason why God invented dictionaries. The simple definition of "permeate" is "occurring throughout." That would not apply in the sentence. The simple definition of "emanate" is "give out, as in breath or an odor." Thus, knowing the right word isn't even always required, which is good for those of us whose memories are on the downward slope of the equation.

> ❖ *Poor choice:* Her rescue by Jeb Krodar, the sheriff of Tannersburg, begins a series of events that change Alice's life.
>
> ❖ *Better choice:* Her rescue by Jeb Krodar, the sheriff of Tannersburg, initiates a series of events that change Alice's life.

Here, we're dealing with the nuance of the word. "Initiates" has a nuance that more clearly expresses the writer's meaning than "begins." ("Sets off " would work.)

> ❖ *Poor choice:* Thank goodness for friends with common experience.
>
> ❖ *Better choice:* Thank goodness for friends with similar experiences.

If the writer really likes the word "common," of course, he can find a way to use it here. "Thank goodness for friends who share a common set of experiences" would work, too.

> ❖ *Poor choice:* My performance over the past year grants this.
>
> ❖ *Better choice:* My performance over the past year merits this.

Again, if the person writing this really likes the word "grants," the sentence can be rearranged to fit that in. "I should be granted this raise, due to my performance over the past year." The problem is rarely a matter of the author clinging to a great word, however, but is usually a question of carelessness and not thinking through the application of the word.

> ❖ *Poor choices:* No sooner did the bridesmaid step into her place at the altar, when the boisterous "dum, dum, de, dum" of the wedding march bounded from the organ.
>
> ❖ *Better choices:* No sooner did the bridesmaid step into her place at the altar, than the boisterous "dum, dum, de, dum" of the wedding march rang out from the organ.

Little words mean a lot—the saying is "No sooner did the something or other **than** the consequent something or other."

And, as for the other misused word here, again, the dictionary shows that "bounded" doesn't quite fit. It doesn't even really fit as a "cute" or "light" word to use in the sentence. By the way, if the author means Mendelssohn's "Wedding March," then the composition title needs to be capitalized and put in quotes.

❖ *Poor choice:* Typical meals for the artist included much the same pattern, with bread and coffee predominating, and with perhaps an occasional carrot or small piece of chicken.

❖ *Better choice:* Typical meals for the artist repeated much the same foods, with bread and coffee predominating, and with perhaps an occasional carrot or small piece of chicken.

Meals don't "include" a "pattern." Here, again, all the author has to do, really, is analyze the word use in a logical fashion.

❖ *Poor choice:* "Stop!" the boy yelled while spurring into action.

❖ *Better choice:* "Stop!" the boy yelled while leaping into action.

We're all a bit fuzzy headed in different respects. Here, I'd say the writer has a vague feeling about "action" that translated into the use of the word "spurring." But the boy in this scene doesn't have a horse, so the association doesn't work. Examine your word use.

❖ *Poor choice:* The leather chair in the corner adds just the right touch of aristocracy.

❖ *Better choice:* The leather chair in the corner adds just the right touch of elegance.

Again, this word selection probably came about because the writer associates the aristocracy with elegance in the home. Words, however, can't be used simply to throw off associations in general in order to create a mood. Each word must be chosen specifically with a conscious understanding of what the word means and how it fits into the sentence.

> ❖ *Poor choice:* You can't retry him again.
>
> ❖ *Better choice:* You can't try him again.
>
> ❖ *Another good choice:* You can't retry him.

You've heard of a double negative; here's a double positive. The word "retry" already contains the "again" part of the statement. Simple, familiar words can be used wrongly, too.

> ❖ *Poor choice:* Your hook should be no larger than a size eight; therefore, the larger the number, the smaller the hook.
>
> ❖ *Better choice:* The larger the number, the smaller the hook. For this type of fish, our hook should be no larger than a size eight.

"Therefore" implies that the situation stated in first independent clause ("Your hook should be no larger than a size eight") above leads to the information in the second clause ("the larger the number, the smaller the hook"). This is obviously not the case, so, here, the logic is faulty.

> ❖ *Poor choice:* Van Gogh's other major source of nutrition leaned toward wine or absinthe.
>
> ❖ *Better choice:* Van Gogh's other major source of nutrition seems to have been wine or absinthe.

A "source" doesn't "lean toward."

These poor choices that don't relate to easily studied rules are tough to correct and lie at the heart of a grave problem for would-be professional writers, students who want to produce writing that works well enough to pass a class, and business people who need to write reports and memos. Regrettably, this isn't a rare difficulty, either. Those who make these types of mistakes are (as the demons inside the poor afflicted fellow in the Bible) legion. One remedy that I *can* suggest is that the writer who struggles with this sort of error eliminates the use of words not well known to her. She can use less of a vocabulary in order to get the writing more nearly right. Any reaching for a word should be done with the help of a dictionary or even a friendly reader able to give accurate feedback.

Common Errors

"Advise" versus "advice"

I often, often, often get notes like this: "Miki, do you have any advise what I should do next to achieve my writing objectives?" I then advise them. Advise is a verb and advice is a noun. They ask for my advice, and I advise them.

Here's a similar one: "The piston corer is an interesting devise."

Obviously, the corer is a device. I'd thus have to conclude that people sometimes confuse the "s" and the "c." If you're one of these people—if you've ever been corrected in this regard—then you must try to get these two letters/sounds straight in your head. And if you can't do that, then you have to use the dictionary each time a word comes up with the sound/letter that confuses you. We don't have to be perfect. We do have to try to understand our flaws and compensate for them. We don't even have to overcome the flaw, you see; all we have to do is make sure it's covered over in public. That's the secret, if not to brilliance, then at least to appearing brilliant. And if you think appearing brilliant isn't more important than being brilliant, ask yourself how long brilliance really lasts. Better yet, ask a senior citizen. The nice thing about the written word is that we can hide a lot of sins between the moment of committing something to paper and the moment of turning the paper in.

"That" versus "who"

This is one that stabs me in the heart every time, which means I get stabbed in a vital organ an awful lot, because people confuse "that" and "who" so consistently that I sometimes feel I learned a different language in my youth than they did.

> ❖ *Wrong:* I do, however, feel a strong attraction to companies who give generous vacation time.
>
> ❖ *Correct:* I do, however, feel a strong attraction to companies that give generous vacation time.
>
> ❖ *Wrong:* The boy that came with me already left.
>
> ❖ *Correct:* The boy who came with me already left.

Companies are entities. They are not persons no matter what the Supreme Court has said. People are represented by the pronoun "who" and companies are represented by the pronoun "that."

"Over" versus "more than"

"Over" is rightfully used to signify "above," as in "The plane flew over the prairie." We generally use "more than" with numbers (or we generally *should* use "more than" with numbers). Sometimes we use "over" with numbers, however.

> ❖ *Correct:* I had more than thirty lottery tickets.
>
> ❖ *Correct:* She's over thirty. I can see it in her face.

"Amongst" versus "among"

I never knew anyone who used the word "amongst" until I began teaching. Then I realized that at least ten percent of the population does. Maybe those using it think that "amongst" sounds fancier than "among." No, it doesn't. However, what the word does sound is archaic. When "thou" returns to common speech, we can bring "amongst" along with it.

"Anxious" versus "eager"

> ❖ *Poor choice:* They were my first clients and I was anxious to gain a good outcome for them.
>
> ❖ *Better choice.* They were my first clients and I was eager to gain a good outcome for them.

We all know what "anxious" means and we all know what "eager" means, so why do we confuse the two in print?

"Said" versus "asked"

> ❖ *Poor choice:* "How have you been, John?" Jim said.
>
> ❖ *Better choice:* "How have you been, John?" Jim asked.

I never saw "said" used for a question, either, until I began teaching. Now the air is rife with "said's" for questions. Is it me? (Or, more properly, "Is it I?")

Words spelled differently are generally different words, but the writer may sometimes confuse the two forms if the spelling of each is similar. Hey, reach for that dictionary. Use the old noggin.

"Compliment" versus "complement"

> ❖ *Correct:* I am happy to compliment you: I like the way your table and chairs complement one another.
>
> ❖ *Correct:* We have a full complement of team members.

If you know how to spell complete, remember the version of the word that has an "e" in the middle—"complement"—implies a form of completion or a form of completeness.

"Than" versus "then"

> ❖ *Correct:* Eric has aged well, looking ten to twelve years younger than his forty-seven years. I remember when he was twenty. He seemed fifteen then.

Than is used to compare and *then* has to do with time.

Many other words have similar spellings and different meanings. Try not to confuse the two forms.

> ❖ *Correct:* At the top of this road is a plain that is full of wild berries. I flew over it in my plane and saw them from above. I plainly had a yen to go berry picking. I like the berries plain, without sugar or cream. I'm going into my garage now to plane some wood with my plane. I exist on a different plane when I work at my crafts.

"Ago" versus "before"

> ❖ *Poor choice:* Charles remembered the last time he had seen his father, three years ago.
>
> ❖ *Better choice:* Charles remembered the last time he had seen his father, three years before.

"Ago" (prior to the present time) puts the reader into relationship with a "now" that can't really be traced from the moment of reading the sentence. If we use, instead, the word "before" (at an earlier time), we shift the sense of time to that of the person or character being discussed.

This doesn't mean that "ago" is always wrong and "before" is always correct in writing. That's not the case. You must examine the point of view of the sentence and whether "prior to the present time" is meant or "at an earlier time."

❖ *Poor choice:* "I went three years before," said Mrs. Reynolds.

❖ *Better choice:* "I went three years ago," said Mrs. Reynolds.

"Toward" versus "towards"

We use "toward" in writing American English. From that, I conclude we also use "backward" rather than "backwards," "downward" instead of "downwards," and so on.

"Such as" versus "like"

In making comparisons, "like" is considered a preposition. Using "like," you can construct a prepositional phrase. "Like" shouldn't be inserted in front of a clause.

❖ *Correct:* He looks like Jack.

❖ *Incorrect:* He looks like he's going hunting.

❖ *Correct:* He looks as if he's going hunting.

I have also seen the statement that "like" is used to compare nouns/pronouns with one another, and that logic often works.

"So" versus "very"

> ❖ *Incorrect:* I was so angry that she kept trying to get me to go with her.
>
> ❖ *Correct:* I was very angry that she kept trying to get me to go with her.

"So" implies a consequence: "I was so angry that I wanted to hit her." Since the first sentence above doesn't include the rest of the expected statement, a different adverb is needed. "Very" doesn't set up a later conclusion, but stands on its own.

"Less" versus "fewer"

> ❖ *Incorrect:* I saw less people in class this week than last.
>
> ❖ *Correct:* I saw fewer people in class this week than last.
>
> ❖ *Correct:* I had less milk to drink than Charlie did.

We use "less" as an adjective with nouns that don't describe countable amounts, but describe quantities—less energy, less food, less alcohol content, less sadness. We use "fewer" with nouns describing that which can be counted—fewer children, fewer pages, fewer thoughts, fewer investments. Of course we have less money than we used to, though we could count and compare. If we counted and compared, we'd find we had fewer dollars. Finally, we go to the shore less frequently than we used to, but in this case, "less" is an adverb, not an adjective. "Fewer" is always an adjective and if we go less frequently to the shore, that really means we go fewer times a year than we used to.

"Healthy" versus "healthful"

I guess the truth can sometimes sound incredible if it shakes your world view. I had a student who refused to believe me on this one. Well, she didn't think differentiating the two words was really necessary. And in some views of language, she might be right. We can slip into the vernacular with hardly anyone being the wiser for it. Those who know the correct use will cringe, however—if only inwardly.

"Healthy" describes a positive state of a living organism or organ—a healthy young lad, a healthy chicken, a healthy heart. The word can even occasionally be used to describe a material object or a concept—a healthy bank account, a healthy imagination. But we can't say a food or supplement or meal is healthy, or that exercise is healthy for you. Green vegetables are healthful in that they promote health in a human being who wants to be healthy. Vitamins are healthful; exercise is a healthful activity. Face what most English-speaking adults already know. These two words are used differently.

Pickup versus pick up

A pickup is a type of truck that is celebrated in country music—or the word could mean a date found on the street. At any rate, the word "pickup" is definitely a noun. "Pick up," however, is a verb. (Or, I might say, a verb and its auxiliary preposition.) We don't pickup the glass or the house or a girl. To acquire any of those we must pick them up. (See why I prefer to call it a verb and its preposition? Because we don't always keep the two parts together, though we should try.)

"Everyday" versus "every day"

Now don't start to think that the *single* word is the noun form, because that isn't so. Here, the single word is an adjective. "He's an everyday kind of guy." The two-word form constitutes a noun and an adjective. "I see him every day." But the form, taken together, here, actually results in adverb. "Every day" modifies "see." That makes "every day" an adverbial, which might, in this case, also be known as an adverbial phrase. Don't shoot the messenger.

"A while" versus "awhile"

> ❖ *Correct:* Stay awhile.
>
> ❖ *Correct:* Stay for a while.

In the first sentence, "awhile" is an adverb that modifies the verb "stay." In the second sentence, the noun "while" is the object of the preposition "for." The phrase "for a while" serves as an adverb. Should you use one form over the other? No. Just know which form you're using and always use the noun when you use the preposition.

"Quote" versus "quotation"

This is one of those controversies that illustrate how our language undergoes transition. Many people insist that the word "quote" is solely a verb, and only the word "quotation" is a noun or, presumably, an adjective, as in "quotation marks." Some sources appear to hold to this view without stating it, while other fine sources mix and match by using both "quotation" and "quote" as nouns. I found "quote" as a noun in eleven dictionaries and then stopped. So do as you will. I use "quote" as a noun as well as an adjective in addition to using it as a verb. I've crossed over on this one.

Quiz

How can you improve your chances of finding and using the right word?

Are the following sentences correct? If not, correct them.

1. His career was long and illustrious.
2. I walked towards the river with him.
3. We had a healthy meal together.
4. Are you fat, floppy, and fed up?
5. I have two less pens then I had yesterday.
6. Burt advised the young man to act like he was enjoying his stay.
7. Did he give her some advise in regard to the contest?
8. I have over one-hundred dollars in the bank.
9. Pills for many health issues have made the pharmaceutical

companies rich.
10. Stephen King, who hails from Maine, has lived there all his life.
11. The odor of spices permeated the house.
12. "Did Charles Dickens write *A Tale of Two Cities?*" the student said.
13. I was so angry at him.
14. The president appears anxious for the tax bill to pass.
15. He is someone that can always get the better of others and that talks big.
16. I feel my hard work grants the raise I'm asking for.
17. She felt intimidated amongst such a crowd.
18. Many people exercise everyday for awhile.
19. That Louis XIV-style furniture adds a touch of royalty to the house.
20. A car and driver go to pickup the reverend's children every afternoon.

Answers

How can you improve your chances of finding and using the right word?

By reading, reading, reading; by using the dictionary; and, in some cases (sadly), by limiting word use.

Are the following sentences correct? If not, correct them.
1. His career was long and illustrious. CORRECT
2. I walked towards the river with him.
   The American version is: "I walked toward the river with him."
3. We had a healthy meal together.
   We had a healthful meal together.
4. Are you fat, floppy, and fed up?
   Are you fat, flabby, and fed up?
5. I have two less pens then I had yesterday.
   I have two fewer pens than I had yesterday.
6. Burt advised the young man to act like he'd enjoyed his stay.
   Burt advised the young man to act as if he'd enjoyed his stay.
7. Did he give her some advise in regard to the contest?
   Did he give her some advice in regard to the contest?

8. I have over one-hundred dollars in the bank.
    I have more than one-hundred dollars in the bank.
9. Pills treating many health issues have made the pharmaceutical companies rich.
    Pills treating many diseases and health complaints have made the pharmaceutical companies rich.
10. Stephen King, who hails from Maine, has lived there all his life.
    Stephen King, who comes from Maine, has lived there all his life.
11. The odor of spices permeated the house. CORRECT
12. "Did Charles Dickens write *A Tale of Two Cities?*" the student said.
    "Did Charles Dickens write A Tale of Two Cities?*" the student asked.*
13. I was so angry at him.
    I was extremely angry at him.
14. The president appears anxious for the tax bill to pass.
    The president appears eager for the tax bill to pass.
15. He is someone that can always get the better of others and that talks big.
    He is someone who can always get the better of others and who talks big.
16. I feel my hard work grants the raise I'm asking for.
    I feel my hard work merits the raise for which I'm asking.
17. She felt intimidated amongst such a crowd.
    She felt intimidated among such a crowd.
18. Many people exercise everyday for awhile.
    Many people exercise every day for a while.
19. That Louis XIV-style furniture adds a touch of royalty to the house.
    That Louis XIV style furniture adds a touch of class to the house.
20. A car and driver go to pickup the reverend's children every afternoon.
    A car and driver go to pick up the reverend's children every afternoon.

Rhythm and Blues

*[B]y listening to the words we can often deduce which
are naturally stressed and find where the rhythm
falters.*

—Gwyneth Box

The best writers know that sentences have a rhythm, that the sound of the words as they combine, the stress on particular syllables, is an important part of the writing. Though written words aren't often meant to be read out loud, they are pronounced internally, and that pronunciation has to be just as metered as a poem.

Creating a proper rhythm in our writing might sound difficult, but achieving the correct rhythm isn't really so hard. Most sentences we write simply fall into a pattern that produces a proper rhythm. Very rarely is writing actually out of an acceptable cadence—and only a relative few writers are off in their rhythm more than from time to time. The rhythm of the writing is a consideration, however, and when the weighting of the words is wrong, the disharmony is readily apparent to an astute reader.

Most frequently when the rhythm of the sentence is missing a beat or two, that means that the sentence doesn't end as strongly as it began, or as it should. That's when we must add words to give the sentence end more oomph, rather than letting the sentence finish flat or trail off. Propping up the final portion of the sentence is so important that this need comes well above the requirement to write efficiently and to have no extraneous words on the page. In instances in which the sentence concludes with a whimper, not a bang, any words that shore up the sentence end—that is, any syllables—are gratefully accepted.

❖ *Weak sentence ends:* Jack was not supposed to be here. While his chest muffled Sandy's screams, her knees gave way, and she fell.

❖ *Improved rhythm:* Jack was not supposed to be here now. While his chest muffled Sandy's horrified screams, her knees gave way beneath her, and she fell.

Here, adding a piece to the penultimate (next to the last) clause changes the rhythm and bolsters the finale by letting it drop away dramatically.

❖ *Weak sentence end:* Betrayed by our biology and confused by the experts, we graze on endless bounties of food while the statistics grow more chilling.

❖ *Improved rhythm:* Betrayed by our biology and confused by the experts, we graze on endless bounties of food while the statistics grow ever more worrisome.

Often when I discuss tacking down the end of a sentence with greater emphasis, I liken this process to the difference between ending a spoken sentence firmly on the downbeat and letting the sentence simply trail off. The writer, very much like the speaker, must transmit a sense of self-confidence and authority, a lack of any doubt. Firm sentence ends send a message of conviction. But take the idea here not as a rule—just as a suggestion. The concept is to watch the sentence rhythm; to be aware that the sentence has a rhythm of which the writer ought to be mindful; and to try to sculpt, improve, and carefully convey all of the elements of the sentence while "selling" the unit as a pitchman sells snake oil.

From time to time, fixing rhythm also means taking away an extra phrase that simply isn't needed.

❖ *Poor rhythm:* Nancy felt her world splinter. And then her heart jolted with a wild thump, leaving her gasping for air.

❖ *Improved rhythm:* Nancy felt her whole world splinter. And then her heart jolted with a wild thump, leaving her gasping.

"Gasping" is a strong word to end on here, much stronger than "for air."

One of the other things we do with the rhythm of the sentence is "punch up" a line. This is especially true in comedic writing.

❖ *Good:* He'd better not even think about laughing.

❖ *Punched up:* He'd better not even consider a laugh.

In the first sentence—*He'd better not even think about laughing*— the reader has to know to emphasize the "think" to make the line work. If the word "think" isn't emphasized, the whole sentence can simply slide by on one tonal level. In the second sentence, the strength of the three-syllable word "consider" forces an earlier emphasis to the line.

The author can also italicize the word "think," which will add power to the word and produce a weighted syllable earlier in the sentence. The problem is in retaining the italic. Some publications to which you might submit ask for no italic or bold, an odd and arrogant mandate for the publisher to set down and yet not entirely unheard of. Of course, the publishing house that asks for manuscripts without italic or bold has a valid point as well. The reader should be the one to choose his own emphasis. At any rate, I like the second sentence above better than the first.

❖ *Not quite the right rhythm:* Delighted that the dog didn't run away from her, Linda walked around the gleaming truck; just as she opened her mouth to announce herself, Herb rose from his crouch.

❖ *Better rhythm:* Delighted that the dog didn't run away from her, Linda walked around the gleaming truck. Then, just as she opened her mouth to announce herself, Herb rose from his crouch.

Here, we use the word "then" like a drum roll to announce the moment and prepare the reader for the punch. Something is going to happen at this point and we suspect, even though we really don't know, that it's going to be a silly or funny event. The rhythm here lets the punchline unfurl.

The above also serves as an example of how punctuation can make a big difference in the way the rhythm will emerge. Separating the two independent clauses and permitting a pause allows the second clause to stand on its own and creates a more emphatic delivery. Using a period and a new sentence slows down the reader so the second clause doesn't slide into the first, losing the emphasis on what's being said.

❖ *Not bad rhythm:* He was about to laugh.

❖ *Better rhythm:* He was going to snicker.

"Snicker" is simply a funnier word than "laugh." But it also adds a syllable, which gives a funny sentence more of a punchline.

❖ *Okay rhythm:* "Welcome," the handsome priest said.

❖ *Better rhythm:* "Welcome," said the handsome priest.

❖ *Flat:* Maybe her condition would pass.

❖ *Better:* She hoped her disturbing state would go away soon.

❖ *Flat:* The words wound down and stopped.

❖ *Better:* The words wound down and finally stopped.

❖ *Flat:* I noticed that the long fingers of his right hand tapped impatiently on his knee.

❖ *Better:* I noticed that the long fingers of his right hand tapped impatiently against his knee.

❖ *Wrong rhythm:* But the darkness that hung in the air was not from lack of light.

❖ *Better rhythm:* But the darkness that hung in the air was not from any lack of light.

❖ *Wrong rhythm:* The boat rocked and pitched in the darkened waters, while the deckhand tugged and coiled the necessary lines.

❖ *Better rhythm:* The boat rocked and pitched in the darkened waters, while the deckhand operated the necessary lines.

You don't want "rocked and pitched" and then "tugged and coiled" because this repeats the same rhythm and will distract readers, who will listen to the sound rather than probe the meaning.

❖ *Flat:* But the group is going to breathe new life into Philadelphia's classical music scene, according to Stone and Richards.

> ❖ *Better:* But the group is going to breathe new life into Philadelphia's classical music scene, according to the two directors.
>
> ❖ *Flat:* I looked over one last time to see how my green friend was faring.
>
> ❖ *Better:* I looked over one last time to see how my green friend was faring on her own.

The question of rhythm has to do with finding a beat that is emphasized. Where is the emphasis here? The last part of the sentence is pretty much on one level. Any emphasis delivered would be from a personal interpretation of the line and not from a syllable rising about the others. If we can find a word to make rise above the others, we might insert that. Otherwise, "on her own" will help.

I hope I've been able to convey something here of what I mean. But commonly the rhythm of a sentence is "off " within the context of several sentences together, or in the field of an entire paragraph. Moreover, as with the comedic writing, sometimes the emotional overtone can be conveyed by the rhythm, an element that also shows up best in context.

Well, what can I do? I can't reproduce an entire few pages right here and point out where, in the middle of things, the writing goes flat. Even if you can't see what I'm remarking on in this section, trust me that I'm making a valuable point.

I'm always quite relieved when a fellow writer comments in regard to paying attention to the rhythm. "You have to," I say enthusiastically in response.

Exercise

The best way to tell if your writing reads well is to read the material out loud. That's a bit time-consuming and might give you a tired throat, but this is the optimal route to take to see how your writing sounds. You're going to catch most of the poor rhythm in that way.

Is that sufficient? As with everything else I point to here, just a dab of effort isn't enough. Reading the piece out loud once is about half of what you need to do. Come back later and read the piece out loud again. Why? Because the mind is like a river, flowing on and producing different reflections of the external world, varied moods. These moods, these biochemical conditions, affect how we are able to perceive. One read-through out loud is good. Two read-throughs are better.

See if you can fix the rhythm on the following:

1. What a contrast between this bright, familiar place and her barren, dark kitchen.
2. Sydney was not supposed to be here.
3. Big fish swam under the boats.
4. Iagor, on board the alien spaceship as it cleared Jupiter and angled for home, looked over to one of his companions.
5. The map refocused on a large expanse of forest that separated the cities.
6. I have traveled there and would never wish to return.
7. And say it in English, not Aramaic. No one actually speaks Aramaic.
8. His head ached and his stomach was not quite right.
9. Fifteen years had aged Jack.
10. When the plane hit an air pocket and dropped several hundred feet, he actually did start praying.
11. The howling from the forest increased in intensity and then stopped.
12. Eyes of muddy green were framed by flesh stretched taut by too many Hershey kisses.
13. Still reeling from the verbal assault, I was in a panic to think of a clever, yet "nice" response.
14. Samuel could only stand there, breathless, able to say nothing.

Suggested fixes

1. What a contrast between this bright, familiar place and her barren, dark kitchen.
   What a contrast between this bright, familiar place and her barren, dark kitchen on Loveless Lane.
2. Sydney was not supposed to be here.
   Sydney was not supposed to be here today.
3. Big fish swam under the boats.
   Big fish swam underneath the boats.

4. Iagor, on board the alien spaceship as it cleared Jupiter and angled for home, looked over to one of his companions.
    Iagor, on board the alien spaceship as it cleared Jupiter and angled for home, looked over to one of his traveling companions.
5. The map refocused on a large expanse of forest that separated the cities.
    The map refocused on a large expanse of forest that separated the metroplexes.
6. I have traveled there and would never wish to return.
    I have traveled there and wouldn't ever desire to return.
7. And say it in English, not Aramaic. No one actually speaks Aramaic.
    And say it in English, not Aramaic. No one actually speaks Aramaic these days.
8. His head ached and his stomach was not quite right.
    His head ached and his stomach still bothered him.
9. Fifteen years had aged Jack.
    The past fifteen years had aged Jack Lambert.
10. When the plane hit an air pocket and dropped several hundred feet, he actually did start praying.
    When the plane hit an air pocket and dropped several hundred feet, he actually did start to pray.
11. The howling from the forest increased in intensity and then stopped.
    The howling from the forest increased in intensity, and then it stopped.
12. Eyes of muddy green were framed by flesh stretched taut by too many Hershey kisses.
    Eyes of muddy green were framed by flesh stretched taut by the eating of too many chocolates.
13. Still reeling from the verbal assault, I was in a panic to think of a clever, yet "nice" response.
    Still reeling from the verbal assault, I was in a panic to think of a clever, yet "nice" response that I might make.
14. Samuel could only stand there, breathless, able to say nothing.
    Samuel could only stand there, breathless, unable to say a single word.

This Goes Here, Because... Well, It Just Does

English is to a large extent an uninflected language. This means that there are very few changeable endings to show us the grammatical function of a word. ...[T]he fact that English is an uninflected language means that the order of words in a sentence must follow a fairly rigid pattern in order to make the meaning clear.

—Paul Shoebottom
English as a second language coordinator,
Frankfurt International School

Although a wrongly positioned word, phrase, or clause isn't the worst goof in the world, the arrangement of elements within a sentence counts. Choosing the layout for the word bits is an underlying part of what we do as writers, even if we don't often talk about this aspect of our process. I notice that I change word positions constantly when I write (thank goodness for word processors). I also often find that newer writers have a less well-developed sense of where this or that belongs.

As with every other component of writing, in positioning pieces of sentences correctly, we must first become conscious that we have choices to make. We must understand that the spot in which we've put a set of words isn't necessarily the optimal location in the sentence for those elements and begin to automatically monitor for that as we write. Then, and only then, do we possess the right psychological outlook to find the best possible place for the word, phrase, or clause.

The proper choice of position for words can't always be explained by way of a rule, but has to do with ease versus awkwardness in our reading of the resulting sentences. I mean, when we mentally, again more or less on autopilot, test variant positionings, some sentence formations will sound natural and some a little clumsy. The ideal choice will usually then become obvious. If the different structures sound about the same to a fairly well-trained ear (yours even), we needn't worry about the sentence any further—or until we come around to the next draft of the piece and something else sounds out of place.

I'm going to enumerate some reasons why certain positioning of sentence parts may be preferable to others and give examples. These concepts are theoretical rather than fixed and rigid rules. But, really, the most important thing is to consider the possibly variable positioning of sentence elements and to train ourselves to simply "know" which sentence composition is better than another. I promise you that each of us is definitely capable of learning this particular skill over time. We might feel ill at ease about our sense of word position for a while, but eventually, we will simply know. This knowing is a function of the biocomputer we each own. For those who want to hurry the process of understanding placement, reading as much really excellent writing as possible helps.

Remember Clarity

❖ *Position that makes the sentence unclear:* She greeted him as he entered without any hugs or kisses.

❖ *Positioning to clarify the sentence:* As he entered, she greeted him without any hugs or kisses.

Ah, the light dawns. She's the one who doesn't reach forward to him. Of course a comma might seem to clarify the sentence slightly—"She greeted him as he entered, without any hugs or kisses," but that really isn't quite clear enough. If the writer places a comma after "entered," we still must pause and muse a bit as to which of them is not hugging or kissing.

Of course, possibly he's the one who doesn't hug or kiss, in which case, the writer must change the statement to something such as: "He entered without an attempt to hug or kiss her, and she stood back, allowing him to avoid an embrace."

❖ *Wrong positioning:* Explorers found licorice root in King Tut's tomb, and ancient warriors quenched their thirst during long marches with it.

❖ *Proper positioning:* Explorers found licorice root in King Tut's tomb, and ancient warriors quenched their thirst with the root during long marches.

In the example here, not only does the idea become scrambled, simply due to the placement of the words "with it" after "marches," but the pronoun "it" doesn't have the proper antecedent, which further adds to the reader's confusion.

Important Facts First

In writing, we use an approach called a set-up. We set up (the verb doesn't have the hyphen) certain facts at the top of a chapter, or section, or paragraph, or even sentence, so when the rest of the ideas are brought in, they already have context. Generally speaking, unless we're trying not to divulge particular information until we are ready to spring such data on the reader, we want to give the most crucial facts up front, in the set-up. This positioning is also a journalistic tenet known as the inverted pyramid, which advocates placing the most crucial details early on in the story, since few readers peruse the entire piece and may not follow the "jump" to another page.

This idea of giving the most important information first applies to the writing of a single sentence. Some instances of how we establish the most vital facts first in that smallest unit of expressing ideas follow.

❖ *Wrong positioning of important information:* The white cloth, spread across the table with care, had bread crumbs all over it after the festive dinner.

❖ *Correct positioning of important information:* After the festive dinner, the white tablecloth no longer appeared quite so pristine. Crumbs of garlic bread and smears of gravy attested to Chef Orlando's preeminent cooking skills.

Yes, I was driven to add some detail. But the important element to note in the context of this chapter is that the dinner is over and done with. How the table looks is therefore a result of everyone having eaten already (and eaten well).

❖ *Wrong positioning of important information:* He took to long walks along the river when they told him he had lung cancer.

❖ *Correct positioning of important information:* After they told him he had lung cancer, he took to long walks along the river.

Our understanding of his walks changes a lot when we know his situation. Don't let us form a wrong impression and then give us information that changes our impression. That will drive the readers crazy.

❖ *Wrong positioning of important information:* Unfortunately, at the university I couldn't get out of science class. Basic biology and chemistry classes were required and research papers were essential for nearly every class to obtain a degree.

❖ *Correct positioning of important information:* Unfortunately, at the university I couldn't get out of taking the sciences. To obtain a degree, basic biology and chemistry classes were required, and research papers were essential for nearly every class.

❖ *Also correct:* Unfortunately, at the university I couldn't get out of taking the sciences. Basic biology and chemistry classes were required to obtain a degree, and research papers were essential for nearly every class.

❖ *Positioning that allows a wrong impression:* My sister, the oldest of the three of us, stands on the other side of me, staring into the water.

❖ *Better positioning:* My sister, the oldest of the three of us, stands on my other side, staring into the water.

We may begin to read "stands on the other side" and think perhaps "the other side of the river." Again, don't let us fashion wrong impressions. The writer must try to get the reader to form the correct image from the get-go.

❖ *Positioning that keeps the reader wondering:* Since she was fifteen years his junior, everyone thought that Ellen would outlive George.

❖ *Better positioning:* Since Ellen was fifteen years George's junior, everyone thought that she would outlive her husband.

Don't make us wonder "who?" for even a nanosecond.

❖ *Awkward positioning:* The agency then submits the resumes of individuals it represents who match these criteria for consideration.

❖ *Smoother positioning:* The agency then submits for consideration the resumes of individuals it represents who match these criteria.

We're saying the resumes are submitted for consideration, not "who match these criteria for consideration."

❖ *Awkward positioning*: Starr Garden's swing sets are erected on the site of the house where W. E. B. Du Bois was born, who wrote *The Souls of Black Folk.*

❖ *Smoother positioning:* Starr Garden's swing sets are erected on the site of the birthplace of W. E. B. Du Bois, author of *The Souls of Black Folk.*

❖ *Also smoother:* Starr Garden's swing sets are erected on the site of the house where W. E. B. Du Bois, who wrote *The Souls of Black Folk*, was born.

And if you want to read some really powerful writing, read *The Souls of Black Folk.* Du Bois neither minces words nor wastes them. You can find the entire text for free, online. Du Bois was a founder of the NAACP.

Modifier and Modified

One common error in positioning is the separation of modifiers from that which they are modifying. Sometimes, yes, we're forced by other priorities to separate a modifier from the modified, but we really should try to keep these elements as close together as possible.

> ❖ *Separation of modifier and modified:* Holding my mallets in one hand, I caught a dribble of sweat with the back of my free hand before it rolled down my nose.
>
> ❖ *Unification of modifier and modified:* Holding my mallets in one hand, with the back of my free hand I caught a dribble of sweat before it rolled down my nose.

We can't have a hand rolling down the person's nose, now can we?

You probably recall (okay, the person picking up this book after you doesn't remember, but I know *you* do) that adverbs can modify a verb, an adjective, or another adverb. A special situation related to the placement of the modifier occurs with adverbs of degree such as *almost, nearly, quite, just, too, enough, hardly, scarcely, completely, very, extremely, frequently, sufficiently, almost, hardly, just, only, even, nearly, especially, particularly, pretty, fairly, rather,* and so on. Two-word negatives such as *not especially, not particularly* also fall within this class. We can notch up the degree or intensity of an action, an adjective or another adverb, or ratchet down the intensity using an adverb of degree. Adverbs of degree are most often placed immediately before the words they modify. Isn't that easy? Well, not entirely, since "enough," which means "to the necessary degree," often goes *after* adjectives and adverbs.

> ❖ *Wrong positioning:* My goal is to increase sales sufficiently enough to generate the income to support my children.
>
> ❖ *Better positioning:* My goal is to sufficiently increase sales to generate enough income to support my children.

❖ *Also good positioning:* My goal is to sufficiently increase sales to generate income enough to support my children.

Happily, this brings up the question of the split infinitive. The phrase "to sufficiently increase" is an example of the split infinitive. The words "to increase" present the infinitive, or most basic form of the verb, and a sort of myth has sprung up that the infinitive must not be broken by an adverb. However, no experts I know of support the view that the infinitive may not be broken. What they do say is that this idea arose from the fact that in Latin the infinitive, which is one word, is never broken. (Well, how do you break a single word?) And many suggest minimizing the frequency with which we split the infinitive. Okkkaaayyy. So long as we can sometimes break the two-word format with an adverb, such as in the example above, I'm willing to comply. Now back to some examples of adverbs of degree:

❖ *Wrong positioning:* I merely said as much as I needed to.

❖ *Better positioning:* I said merely as much as I needed to.

❖ *Wrong positioning:* I just wanted a few carrots.

❖ *Better positioning:* I wanted just a few carrots.

"Just" is a word we use quite a bit; therefore, we should take special care to position the word right before the term it modifies when possible. (In fact, this is a word we should do a special search on because many writers tend to *over*use the "just.") Then, too, sometimes adverb placement—degree or whatever— is up to the author.

> ❖ Optional positioning: She frequently went.
>
> ❖ Optional, though probably better positioning: She went frequently.

Other types of adverbs you never heard of anyway not only exist but have rules affecting their sentence positions. Let me just mention them here to be somewhat tormenting (heh heh). *Adverbs of manner,* which indicate the *way* in which something happens—*fast, slowly, softly, gently*—are usually placed after the verb or after the object: *I went fast. She drew the picture nicely.* We wouldn't say: *I fast went. She nicely drew the picture.*

Adverbs of time (when *and* duration)—*now, then, for a day, for a year*—often go at the end of a sentence. *Adverbs of frequency* (*always, never*) indicate approximately how many times something happens and are placed at the end of a sentence, after the main verb, or after a verb auxiliary. *Adverbs of place* tell us where an incident happens or takes place (*anywhere, there, downstairs*) and are positioned after the main verb, after the object, or at the beginning of the sentence.

And what about *adverbs of certainty (undoubtedly, certainly)*? *Adverbs of attitude* (*frankly, seriously*)? Oh, come on. The rules here are so pieced together that we might as well go by our own best, considered judgment—the key word being "considered."

A Verb and Its Ancillary

I mentioned this idea before without making a fuss over the concept. Let me point to it more strongly here. We should try to keep the ancillary with its verb. This isn't always possible, but for the sake of having an exemplary writing style, we ought to try.

> ❖ *Could be better:* He pried the jar open.
>
> ❖ *Better:* He pried open the jar.
>
> ❖ *Could be better:* I revved the engine up.

❖ *Better:* I revved up the engine.

❖ *Could be better:* They invited the kids in.

❖ *Better:* They invited in the kids.

Don't Interrupt

Some positioning problems have to do with the interruption of ideas. Don't interrupt an idea in the middle of presenting it in order to insert another idea. Finish an idea, then go on to the next.

❖ *Positioning that interrupts the idea:* She saw through the one-way mirror separating the shop and the office how her father dealt with his clients.

❖ *Positioning that presents one idea, then the next:* Through the one-way mirror separating the shop and the office, she saw how her father dealt with his clients.

❖ *Positioning that interrupts the idea:* Her short black hair is spiky because every time she is upset or angry, she runs her hands through her hair. Which is pretty much every day.

❖ *Positioning that presents one idea, then the next:* Her short black hair is spiky because every time she is upset or angry, which is pretty much every day, she runs her hands through her hair.

You can see from the example here that an "idea" doesn't have to be anything intellectual or belabored, but may be a simple, brief thought or part of a thought. Present the complete concept and then go on. You don't want to scramble what you're writing, darting here and there, hitting the reader with fragments of thoughts instead of creating a cohesive whole that flows in logical sequence.

The reason I can't say that any of the above are rules is that we can't differentiate the rationales for word position adequately. The sense that we're separating the modifier from that which it modifies may really be the same thing as interrupting an idea. So, really, any of these arguments that strike you in trying to "figure out" the position of sentence elements can work if they appeal to your own personal logic.

Here are some more examples:

❖ *Wrong positioning:* I know a lot of mothers who write with young children—even multiple young children.

❖ *Better positioning:* I know a lot of mothers with young children—even several young children—who write.

They shouldn't use young children to write. Really! A pen or keyboard works better.

❖ *Wrong positioning:* Ed and Jack were more stumbling than walking.

❖ *Better positioning:* Ed and Jack were stumbling more than walking.

❖ *Better sentence:* Ed and Jack stumbled more than they walked.

❖ *Wrong positioning:* She heard her mother's voice approaching behind her, vaguely irritated.

❖ *Better positioning:* She heard her mother approaching behind her, speaking in a vaguely irritated tone.

Okay, this sentence was a mess. The mother's disembodied voice wasn't approaching.

> ❖ *Wrong positioning:* Her father very patiently explained the concept of an arranged marriage to her.
>
> ❖ *Better positioning:* Her father very patiently explained to her the concept of an arranged marriage.

After all, not all arranged marriages can be to her.

> ❖ *Wrong positioning:* Employees would also like a platform to present any concerns they may have in a confidential manner.
>
> ❖ *Better positioning:* Employees would also like a platform to present in a confidential manner any concerns they may have.

Once again I find myself recommending the reading of fine literature as a way to facilitate the absorption of good writing habits. That's the way we burn templates for good writing into our nervous systems.

Exercise

Correct the following:

1. She touched John's arm again, then pushed the door to ICU-4 open and went inside.
2. Teamed up with my curiosity, my feet stopped me in front of the band placement list after the crowd cleared.
3. Yup, that was Jane, up to her old trick of interacting (however covertly) with the public, something she loves to do just for fun.
4. Jerry turned on his side to avoid the child's stare, but his left arm fell asleep quickly.
5. She recalled vaguely retrieving her car from the valet parking attendant outside the hotel.
6. Max Franz returns my hug stiffly.
7. Some employers recruit through campus career centers for

summer internships.

8. Driving in the opposite direction, a man with a bushy mustache pulled his dented car over to the opposite curb.
9. While there, Lori spots a ship (*The Water Lily*) on the riverbank that catches her fancy.
10. Sara never intends to marry, but she establishes a warm relationship with Henry, the lawyer handling her father's affairs, via e-mail, believing him to be elderly.
11. I began to communicate with a few actors I admired and respected via e-mail and personal messages.
12. Reality was an adult world of failed relationships, and so I retreated into a genre of mystery novels, filled with murderers and social deviants, by Agatha Christie.

Possible Corrections

1. She touched John's arm again, then pushed the door to ICU-4 open and went inside.
   She touched John's arm again, then pushed open the door to ICU-4 and went inside.
2. Teamed up with my curiosity, my feet stopped me in front of the band placement list after the crowd cleared.
   After the crowd cleared, my feet stopped me in front of the band placement list.
3. Yup, that was Jane, up to her old trick of interacting (however covertly) with the public, something she loves to do just for fun.
   Yup, that was Jane, up to her old trick of interacting with the public (however covertly), something she loves to do just for fun.
4. Jerry turned on his side to avoid the child's stare, but his left arm fell asleep quickly.
   Jerry turned on his side to avoid the child's stare, but his left arm quickly fell asleep.
5. She recalled vaguely retrieving her car from the valet parking attendant outside the hotel.
   She vaguely recalled retrieving her car from the valet parking attendant outside the hotel.
6. Max Franz returns my hug stiffly.
   Max Franz stiffly returns my hug.

7. Some employers recruit through campus career centers for summer internships.
   Some employers recruit for summer internships through campus career centers.
8. Driving in the opposite direction, a man with a bushy mustache pulled his dented car over to the opposite curb.
   Driving his car in the opposite direction, a man with a bushy mustache pulled over to the opposite curb.
9. While there, Lori spots a ship (*The Water Lily*) on the riverbank that catches her fancy.
   *While there, Lori spots on the riverbank a ship (*The Water Lily*) that catches her fancy.*
10. Sara never intends to marry, but she establishes a warm relationship with Henry, the lawyer handling her father's affairs, via e-mail, believing him to be elderly.
    Sara intends never to marry, but she establishes a warm relationship via e-mail with Henry, the lawyer handling her father's affairs, believing him to be elderly.
11. I began to communicate with a few actors I admired and respected via email and personal messages.
    I began to communicate via email and personal messages with a few actors I admired and respected.
12. Reality was an adult world of failed relationships, and so I retreated into a genre of mystery novels filled with murderers and social deviants, by Agatha Christie.
    Reality was an adult world of failed relationship, and so I retreated into Agatha Christie novels, filled with murderers and social deviants.

Quite Amazing Adjectives, Especially Astounding Adverbs

*An adjective habit, or a wordy, diffuse, flowery habit,
once fastened upon a person, is as hard to get rid of
as any other vice.*

—Mark Twain

*"There's the agent now!... I'm going to speak to
him!" impulsively declared Ned.*
—from Tom Swift and His Great Searchlight

*The poet is supposed to be the person who can't get
enough of words like "incarnadine." This was not my
experience.*

—*Louise Gluck*
appointed U.S. poet laureate in 2003

I guess what I'm expected to do after those quotes is rail against the use of adjectives and adverbs. Not a chance. I admire cunning adjectives. I crave piquantly rousing adverbs. What writer, secretly, in his heart of hearts doesn't worship such delectables? Of course, excess in modification exceeds moderation. Let's admit right now that too much is actually, ah… too much. Don't use too much modification, but, then again, sometimes modifiers are needed.

Really, adjectives aren't the ones to blame. The one causing all the trouble is the writer who is focused more on amping up the words than on transmitting meaning. Our job as writers is to convey content. If we do that with pleasing words, that's to the good, but content is king.

Adjectives are often required in order to describe. Specific description helps the reader to *see* the object of the article or story's focus. Let's describe as required, while forwarding the goal of communication, and let's not simply aim at producing the words.

Occasionally I will mark a person's assignment with the word "adjective" before a noun. This might be for the rhythm of the sentence, in fact, but sometimes we do simply need a description of any type to enliven the material. We should write economically and count the adjectives in our word banks as if they were cash, but I hope we won't be downright stingy, parsimoniously allowing our nouns to do without a little modest decoration.

Compounding Adjectives

I now want to discuss adjective hyphenation. That's the real mystery of the adjectives, how they become compounds. I like this quote from Sonia Jaffe Robbins at New York University: "Hyphens cause writers more trouble than any other form of punctuation, except perhaps commas. This may be because the hyphen has no analogue in speech; it is punctuation created purely by the needs of print." That says it all. Well, not all, for I'll forge on—as does Ms. Robbins.

The point she makes (I'm making this point here, too, so don't forget about me) is that some words take a hyphen when joined with an adjective: *well, self, quasi, half, all, ill, better, best, little, pro, co, anti*, and such.

But some of these compounds only take the hyphen when they come before the noun: well-liked teacher, the teacher is well liked; an ill-suited suitor, her suitor is ill suited; a better-known book, this book is better known.

And some take the hyphen wherever they are: quasi-intellectual content, the content is quasi-intellectual; half-witted students, the students are half-witted; a self-respecting employee, the employee is self-respecting.

Watch out for other phrases that shouldn't be hyphenated.

> ❖ *Incorrect:* He kept his records up-to-date.
>
> ❖ *Correct:* He kept his records up to date.

❖ *Correct:* He kept up-to-date records.

❖ *Incorrect:* The records were up-to-date.

❖ *Correct:* The records were up to date.

In the first example pair, "up to date" is an adverb that refers to the way in which he keeps his records. We can, however, say specifically that the records are themselves "up-to-date," using the phrase as an adjective ("up-to-date records"), and before the noun, the hyphens are correct. But even if we use a linking verb and "up to date" is an adjective ("were up to date"), when the adjective phrase is used after the noun, we don't employ hyphens. Speaking of adverb hyphenation, we don't use a hyphen with an "ly" word.

❖ *Incorrect:* A highly-connected candidate is likely to be elected.

❖ *Correct:* A highly connected candidate is likely to be elected.

Continual mistakes in employing—or not employing—compound words is a sign that a writer doesn't know the language well. Compound words are either two words, hyphenated, or one word made from two. "Bunkhouse" is correct, and "bunk house" or "bunk-house" is incorrect, though we won't get a razz from the spellchecker with "bunk house" or "bunk-house"—the spellchecker doesn't know our intention with the words. What we can do when we're suspicious that our use of two words is wrong is spell the word as one and see if the spellchecker thinks that's okay. Then, again, we can open up the actual dictionary, also considered a useful tool.

Trust me when I say that incorrectly joining words and incorrectly separating them are very eyebrow-raising errors, if the reader is at all sophisticated. Take the time to look up the word/words/expression. I'm lazy and I use the dictionary when I need to. So can you.

Before moving on to discuss questions of adverbs, let's look at the compound adjective that we put together for one-time use.

> ❖ *Correct:* The spice scented steam drifted upward, toward her face.
>
> ❖ *Better:* The spice-scented steam drifted upward, toward her face.

The so-called rule mandating the hyphen in a compound adjective should serve simply as a guideline. Okay, we do have an absolute. The rule is to insert the hyphen when that will aid in reader comprehension. Does the hyphen here improve our understanding of the sentence? In other words, the choice is up to the person composing the sentence. We must use our own best judgment. But first we have to develop good judgment. That takes a while.

Many compound words with numbers take hyphens, such as in "a fifteen-year-old boy." Often I see "a fifteen-year old boy," which is incorrect. We must use both hyphens. We also hyphenate "a fifteen-year-old" when "old" is the substitute noun.

Cursing Adverbs

Most people in the world would never tell you that the use of the adverb is ill advised. But a certain group of "wise" writers might try to. They've gotten the "rule" from mystery author Elmore Leonard, and the advice has spread from the mystery writing community to groups of other genre writers. I like Elmore Leonard; I interviewed him for my book on writing mysteries. He's a very nice man, very agreeable, and a good writer, too. But this idea of eschewing the adverb has got to go.

What's wrong with the adverb? Only one thing. We should be careful in using too many "ly" words near one another. The problem with adverbs is a problem with the repeated "ly" sound, and that's the whole tempest in a teacup right there. We ought to use our "ly" words sparingly and not in close proximity. Period. Anything else is too completely silly to even contemplate. Those who say we must cut our adverbs (to spite our faces) don't have a problem with an adverb phrase or clause, or even an adverb modifying an adjective. But they don't understand that they actually approve of adverbs because they aren't using the old thinking cap very well.

Elmore Leonard's style is Elmore Leonard's style. He's a sincere, committed, and honest writer. But not every writer has to sound like Elmore Leonard. Let's stop denigrating the noble servant of so many parts of speech (the adverb slaves over the verb, the adjective, and its own fellow adverbs). Give the adverb its due— respect and honor. Go, adverb babies, go. Or maybe that's "Go softly, adverb babies, go with care."

Adverb *vs.* Adjective

The rough stuff comes into play at this spot. Adverbs and adjectives duke it out, which, like all scrapping between siblings, is really ridiculous. Why are they at odds? Each has its job. What's the problem?

The problem, as it usually does, comes down to humans. Humans create the difficulties, not two perfectly decent, rule-abiding parts of speech. People! People get confused as to which modifier should be used where (when?). People forget to use logic. They forget to analyze which other part of speech is being catered to and to use that as the basis for picking the modifier. One tricky aspect of choosing a modifier comes into play when we have a linking verb. The linking verb links the subject with an adjective modifier.

❖ *Correct:* That sweater looks good on you.

❖ *Correct:* I feel good. ("Well" can also be used as an adjective when related to health.)

❖ *Correct:* The food tastes good.

Those are all linking verbs that link the modifier, an adjective, with the subject. But those same verbs can be action verbs and take an adverb.

❖ *Correct:* The boy looked fondly at his mother.

❖ *Correct:* I carefully feel the fabric before buying dress material.

❖ *Correct:* The dog enthusiastically tasted the chicken.

Not all adverbs use an "ly" ending. *Very, fast* (also used as an adjective), *quite, so, almost, never,* and *less* are adverbs. At the same time, some adjectives end in "ly"—*lovely, friendly, lonely,* and *neighborly,* for instance. Some few adverbs have more than one form, such as *late/lately.* Clauses can also be used as adverbs, as can phrases of different types.

❖ *Clause as adverb:* After I catch him, I'm going to kill him.

❖ *Prepositional phrase as adverb:* He scurried under the turnstile.

❖ *Infinitive phrase as adverb:* He tried to forget her.

❖ *As...as phrase as adverb:* He went to the movies as recently as yesterday.

Comparatives and Superlatives

Comparatives and superlatives are modifiers that show degrees. The regular form of the comparative adjective takes an "er," while the regular form of the superlative adjective adds an "est." Adjectives that have irregular forms include *good,* better, best; *bad,* worse, worst; *less,* lesser, least; and *many,* more, most. Adverbs can show comparison as well. The comparative of most adverbs adds the word "more," while the superlative adds the word "most." Adverb comparative and superlatives can be irregular, too: *well,* better, best; *badly,* worse, worst; and *ill,* worse, worst.

Some adjectives and adverbs don't have comparative and superlative forms because they already express the ultimate degree: *fatal*, *favorite*, and *empty* are examples of that type of ultimate adjective. The problem here, again, is in distinguishing whether to use the adjective or the adverb. A pause to decide what part of speech is being modified is in order.

> ❖ *Incorrect:* He ran quicker than Melvin.
>
> ❖ *Correct:* He ran more quickly than Melvin.
>
> ❖ *Incorrect:* Of his field, he ran the quickest.
>
> ❖ *Correct:* Of his field, he ran the most quickly.

Here, in both instances, the verb is being modified, so we use the adverb. Mistakenly using the adjective instead of the adverb is the most frequent error in this type of formation.

Quiz

1. What's the rule for creating compound adjectives?
2. What's the trend with hyphens?
3. What's wrong with adverbs?
4. What do comparatives and superlatives do?
5. What's the comparative of fatal?

Exercise

Fix the following. Mark any that are correct as correct.

1. He gave us the news up-to-the-moment.
2. He gave us news that was up-to-the-moment.
3. He gave us up-to-the-moment news.
4. Leonore was a well-liked teacher and happy that she was well-liked.
5. We enjoy dinner-theatre on a monthly basis in the summer.
6. He hurried quicker than a goose protecting her chicks.
7. He was the best singer of the two finalists.
8. My cold is gone and I feel pretty well today.

9. My cold is gone and I feel pretty good today.
10. The sweater feels comfortably on me.
11. That's a beautifully-designed sweater.
12. She has a twelve-year old son.
13. We went up in a hot-air balloon.
14. They bought cinnamon scented candles.
15. They were the better skaters of any of the competitors.

Answers
Quiz

1. What's the rule for creating compound adjectives?
   The rule is to create compound adjectives when that will help the reader's comprehension.
2. What's the trend with hyphens?
   The trend is away from hyphens, but that may be because writers are afraid of them. Hyphens are a good thing, and sophisticated readers appreciate their use.
3. What's wrong with adverbs?
   Nothing. The only problem is having "ly" sounds close together, as repeats. Watch those.
4. 4. What do comparatives and superlatives do?
   Comparatives compare (only two elements) and superlatives extol one above all others.
5. What's the comparative of fatal?
   Fatal is one of those words that has no comparative or superlative.

Exercise

1. He gave us the news up-to-the-moment.
   He gave us the news up to the moment. (We don't hyphenate the adverb.)
2. He gave us news that was up-to-the-moment.
   He gave us news that was up to the moment. (With the linking verb, this is an adjective phrase, but we don't hyphenate it when it comes after the noun.)
3. He gave us up-to-the-moment news. *Correct.*
4. Leonore was a well-liked teacher and happy that she was well-liked.
   Leonore was a well-liked teacher and happy that she was well

liked.
(After the noun, we don't hyphenate an adjective formed with "well.")

5. We enjoy dinner-theatre on a monthly basis in the summer.
   We enjoy dinner theatre on a monthly basis in the summer.
6. He hurried quicker than a goose protecting her chicks.
   He hurried more quickly than a goose protecting her chicks. (This is a comparison of two. "More quickly" is an adverb phrase modifying "hurried.")
7. He was the best singer of the two finalists.
   He was the better singer of the two finalists.
8. My cold is gone, and I feel pretty well today.
   Correct—we sometimes use "well" as an adjective with the linking verb when we refer to health.
9. My cold is gone, and I feel pretty good today.
   Correct. We use an adjective with a linking verb.
10. The sweater feels comfortably on me.
    The sweater feels comfortable on me. (The verb is linking and takes an adjective.)
11. That's a beautifully-designed sweater.
    That's a beautifully designed sweater. (No hyphen with an "ly" adverb.)
12. She has a twelve-year old son.
    She has a twelve-year-old son.
13. We went up in a hot-air balloon.
    Correct with or without the hyphen.
14. They bought cinnamon scented candles.
    Correct with or without the hyphen. I prefer the hyphen here.
15. They were the better skaters of any of the competitors.
    They were the best skaters of any of the competitors.

Time Travel With Verbs

The verbs in English are a fright.
How can we learn to read and write?
Today we speak, but first we spoke;
some faucets leak, but never loke.
If I still do as once I did,
Then do cows moo, as they once mid?

—Richard Lederer

Although Einstein proposed, and other scientists have since proven, that time is actually relative to how fast we ourselves are traveling in space, here on Earth we have some pretty fixed concepts regarding past, present, and future. Luckily for those of us who share the English language, our verbs are able to denote just about every aspect of time that our generally rigid primate minds can envision. Using the right form (also known as tense) is the effortful part of the equation.

Some verbs are "regular," which means they are generally put together by a set of rules that is predictable: The verbs are each "conjugated" (put into the various tenses) in much the same fashion. Other verbs are irregular: Yet, still, native English speakers may conjugate the most far-out, irregular verbs with nary a stumble—as with the "to be" verb: I am, you are, he/she/it is, we are, you are, they are, and the whole range of rather wild tense variations.

These irregulars beat in our pulses. To most of us, they are simple. (If they aren't simple to you, though, get an irregular verb dictionary or find a table of their conjugations online. Double check every time you use the verb.)

Some few irregular verbs, however, cause many even an educated writer a whole bunch of difficulty: The two verbs *lay* (to put or place) and *lie* (to recline), for instance, are often mistaken one for the other, and people slip up horrendously with each.

Past Tense Rules

Most work is written in past tense. I want to let that sentence stand on its own because I'd like that fact to sink in a bit. The great bulk of writing in our language is in past tense. But inevitably at least half of the students in my fundamentals classes begin their writing experimentations in present tense. I don't know why.

I have an eerie feeling when I read these pieces, and that mood, a sense of the surreal, is perhaps the reason why readers don't much like to read in present tense. Yet even as I say that, you will pick up a literary magazine, and voila, find a couple of stories in present tense. Yes, present tense is thought to be literary. Why? Maybe because that twilight-zone feeling that the present tense evokes is considered "cool." The reader feels sort of weirded out and goes, "Wow, literary. Great writing." (Present tense is used extensively in new adult category novels, however, and sometimes in young adult novels.)

Actually, I exaggerate a little because in the ordinary course of writing events we do some work in the present tense. I have written for publications in which all the verbs of citation are given in present tense, and from time to time I deliberately write an article that way to make the occurrences seem more immediate.

By the way, I'm writing this material in the present tense, too, yet you don't feel all peculiar in your stomach, do you? No. That's because I'm writing something that continues to be true and isn't finished after it's written. However, my strongest advice to writers is to write in past tense and try to stay there. Once you've written the piece, go over it a few times, and during one pass simply make sure you've been consistent in your use of tense. Don't move back and forth from past to present, tensewise. That definitely addles our readers' brains.

Sometimes in English, despite the fact that we're writing in past tense, we will come to a point at which we make a statement in present tense. That may be okay for some uses, and for other uses we might want to translate those sentences into past tense.

❖ *Correct:* I live near the State Office Building on 125th Street, and passing by, I noticed that a concert had begun on the plaza.

❖ *Better:* I lived near the State Office Building on 125th Street, and passing by, I noticed that a concert had begun on the plaza.

I do live near that building (that's the exact name of the building so I capitalize it). But suppose tomorrow I moved to an apartment in Trump Towers, and the day after that my piece came out in a newspaper, saying where I live and giving the wrong data about my location. Any type of information that might be transitory, including information that seems fairly stable—"West Street lies west of East Street"—should be put in past tense if that's otherwise consistent with the material. "West Street lay west of East Street" would be correct because in ten years, the city might come in and change the names of the streets. Farfetched? Yes, but this is a way to understand how we use the verbs, especially in fiction. On the other hand, we do maintain present tense for some types of statements that seem as if they will be forever true. "The Statue of Liberty stands in New York Harbor." Of course, nothing in the universe is permanent, but we act—and write—as if some things are failsafe. We would like to think that Lady Liberty will always stand where she does at exactly this minute. At any rate, by minimizing what we regard as permanent, we lessen the amount of toggling back and forth between past and present that we must do.

Progressive Forms

We want our verbs to be strong ones that give a dynamic feel to our writing, even if we are lazy layabouts personally. One way we can intensify our verbs is to avoid using the progressive when we don't need to.

What's the progressive? The progressive (also known as "continuous") represents a continuing action, and, of course, sometimes we need to provide that effect. But if we can minimize the use, we confer a more vibrant feel on our work.

❖ *Correct:* When people were building homes here in the late 1800s, the subway had not yet provided general access to the area.

❖ *Better:* When people built homes here in the late 1800s, the subway had not yet provided general access to the area.

❖ *Correct:* She was beginning to get angry.

❖ *Better:* She had begun to get angry.

The "to be" verb is a great boon to our language, but the various forms of the verb can seem weak and are often repeated, bringing further weakness to the writing. I frequently mark students' sentences with "Use the most direct verb possible," as well as "Minimize your use of the 'was.' " The past perfect "had begun" is more effective a verb than "was beginning" and serves as a possible alternative when the simple past tense doesn't seem exactly right. In general, we do, indeed, want to limit the "was" form.

❖ *Correct:* The dog was back for more.

❖ *Better:* The dog came back for more.

Another weak verb is "get."

❖ *Correct:* The dog's growling got louder.

❖ *Better:* The dog's growling rose in volume.

Strong verbs, if they are still appropriate to a sentence and if they don't draw an amount of attention to themselves that overwhelms the rest of the sentence, serve our writing better than weaker verbs.

Past Perfect

The past perfect, also known to a few intimate friends as "pluperfect," consists of two parts: a form of the verb "to have" and the past participle of the verb being set into the past perfect. Past perfect is used to discuss an event completed before another action written about in past tense. "I had gone there with John yesterday. Today I went with Ralph, but not without feeling rather dishonest." (Present perfect expresses an action begun in the past that isn't yet done with: *"I've tried to be a good husband," he said. Well, okay, he has tried.*)

Past perfect is a tense I feel strongly about. Many writers omit the past perfect or say they've been told they needn't use it or they only must use it once in a paragraph, or some similar silliness. I become pretty agitated about such things.

My statement on the use of the past perfect is: If the past perfect is called for, then use it. Pretty fierce, huh? And I mean it, too. I'm strict, but I'm fair.

Contractions

I told the publisher I might skip verbs. "They're pretty important, aren't they?" he asked, Zen-like. Ummm. Yeah, I guess. But these few pages are about all I have to say concerning verbs. Verb contractions used correctly are good; used incorrectly, they're bad.

> ❖ *Correct:* Jane could not breathe.
>
> ❖ *Better:* Jane couldn't breathe.

The use of contractions makes the writing sound more natural.

> ❖ *Incorrect:* Composers expected musicians to be creative, to spring off from what's on the page.

> ❖ *Correct:* Composers expected musicians to be creative, to spring off from what was on the page.

The contraction "what's" stands for "what is," but here the writer wants to say "what was." The only way to say "what was" is to use those exact words.

Exercise

Correct the following, making the verbs consistent.

In one company project that will run recently, reps who were RNs go into physicians' offices and have talked to their counterparts about dealing with asthma on a more proactive basis according to evidence-based, medical guidelines. They would help the staff understood the type of patients who benefits from a more aggressive approach using *control* medications, rather than *rescue* medications. The nurse reps will encourage and informed the office staff about proactive treatment so that the staff nurses could suggested to the physicians that getting a specific patient on a controller medication might was a good idea.

Quiz

Correct the following:

1. She saw him lie the book on the table, then she laid down to rest.
2. We drove south to the ruins, where locals peddle their souvenirs.
3. The soldiers are training in the States before being sent overseas.
4. Our tour guides did not seem to rest.
5. The children got close to the fence, then stopped.
6. They wanted to know who's going last week.
7. Although Mrs. Wilson shopped yesterday, she shopped again today.
8. The architects were planning those homes for purchase by the wealthy of the time.
9. Eleanor Roosevelt goes to the window and looks out on her garden.
10. The Statue of Liberty stood in New York Harbor.

Answers

Exercise

In one project that ran recently, reps who were RNs went into physicians' offices and talked to their counterparts about dealing with asthma on a more proactive basis according to evidence- based, medical guidelines. They helped the staff understand the type of patients who would benefit from a more aggressive approach using *control* medications, rather than *rescue* medications. The nurse reps encouraged and informed the office staff about proactive treatment so that the staff nurses could suggest to the physicians that getting a specific patient on a controller medication might be a good idea.

Quiz

1. She saw him lie the book on the table, then she laid down to rest.
   She saw him lay the book on the table, then she lay down to rest.
2. We drove south to the ruins, where locals peddle their souvenirs.
   We drove south to the ruins, where locals peddled their souvenirs.
3. The soldiers are training in the States before being sent overseas.
   The soldiers train in the States before being sent overseas.
4. Our tour guides did not seem to rest.
   Our tour guides didn't seem to rest.
5. The children got close to the fence, then stopped.
   The children approached the fence, then stopped.
6. They wanted to know who's going last week.
   They wanted to know who was going last week.
7. Although Mrs. Wilson shopped yesterday, she shopped again today.
   Although Mrs. Wilson had shopped yesterday, she shopped again today.
8. The architects were planning those homes for purchase by the wealthy of the time.

The architects planned those homes for purchase by the wealthy of the time.

9. Eleanor Roosevelt goes to the window and looks out on her garden.

   Correct, but I'm discombobulated at thinking of Mrs. Roosevelt in the present tense.

10. The Statue of Liberty stood in New York Harbor.

    The Statue of Liberty stands in New York Harbor. (Unless this is a science fiction piece.)

PART III

Put It Together

How Long Should a Sentence Be?

Part of the writer's task is to employ whatever music is available to him or her in language, and part of language's music lies within the rhythms of varied sentence length and structure. Even poets who write within the formal limits and sameness of an iambic pentameter... will sometimes strike a chord against that beat and vary the structure of their clauses and sentence length, thus keeping the text alive and the reader awake.

—The Guide to Grammar and Writing
Capital Community College Foundation,
www.ccc.commnet.edu/grammar/

Sometimes I tell students to combine sentences for efficiency, and sometimes I tell them to divide a single sentence into two. How can we know when we should merge a sentence with another, or when we should cut a sentence into independent clauses? This depends on how the sentence reads *in situ*—that is, how the words strike our inner ears in the context of all the sentences around the one under construction.

Often, as a reader, if I see a string of simple declarative sentences, I want a couple of complex sentences thrown into the mix. Or if I notice sentences with vague "There were" or "It was" openings, I suspect at once that the sentences aren't replete with ideas and can be combined with nearby pieces for a more interesting, fuller sentence structure.

Conversely, if I find myself getting dizzy or running out of breath, or forgetting what the opening was within the length of a single sentence, I know that the sentence has gotten out of hand. The writer needs to call a halt to the words and trim radically or simply use a "period capital" to cut the piece in two.

Here are some examples of combining as well as cutting to build better sentences.

With No New Subject

> ❖ *Mediocre structure:* The property is referred to as a ranch. There are ninety acres of bushland and plenty of lake front.
>
> ❖ *Better structure:* The property, referred to as a ranch, comprises ninety acres of bushland and extensive lake front.

Unless you have a reason to create a new sentence—a different subject or an exciting verb—stick with a single structure. On the other hand, you might have a reason to both put sentences together and cut them in two at the same time (holy moly!).

> ❖ *Mediocre structure:* The property is referred to as a ranch. There are ninety acres of bushland and plenty of lake front that could be developed as a year-round hunting or fishing resort with cabins.
>
> ❖ *Better structure*: The property, referred to as a ranch, comprises ninety acres of bushland and plenty of lake front that could be developed as a year-round hunting or fishing resort with cabins.
>
> ❖ *Better structure still:* The property, referred to as a ranch, comprises ninety acres of bushland and plenty of lake front. The extensive lot could be developed as a year-round hunting or fishing resort with cabins.

Sometimes, as I mention above, we want to combine sentences to make a more interesting structure in the midst of too many short, choppy sentences.

❖ *Choppy structure:* My room was a mess. Laundry was strewn about. Books and papers were lying on my unmade bed.

❖ *Single, unified structure:* My room was a mess with laundry strewn about and books and papers lying on my unmade bed.

In changing these three sentences to one, we also get rid of the weak "was" helper verb. And let's not bother to repeat a subject when we have short sentences that can be combined.

❖ *Redundant structure:* He donned the nearest shirt and trousers he could find. He licked his fingers and ran them over his head.

❖ *Improved structure:* He donned the nearest shirt and trousers he could find, then licked his fingers and ran them over his head for neatness' sake.

❖ *Redundant structure:* I was tired. I hadn't slept in days.

❖ *Improved structure:* Not having slept in days, I was tired.

Remember to place the information we need most first. Surely "not having slept in days" is important to the reader's understanding "was tired."

❖ *Redundant structure:* Working together, we were able to uncover what turned out to be an old suitcase. It was

---

> a red leather suitcase with a handle and locks on either side.
>
> ❖ *Improved structure:* Working together, we were able to uncover what turned out to be an old red leather suitcase.

Speaking of redundant, don't all suitcases have handles and locks? And what does "on either side" mean, anyway? On either side of what? What is really meant is "a handle, with locks on either side of the handle." If we don't specify, we could mean with a handle on one side of the suitcase and the locks on the other side. But that isn't how suitcases are manufactured. If we drop the entire phrase, we don't have to go into the minutia concerning suitcase construction, which doesn't enlighten the reader, anyway.

> ❖ *Poor structure:* Ted Bundy served as his own defense attorney. He was moved to Miami for his trial, as he felt it would be difficult to find an impartial jury in northern Florida.
>
> ❖ *Better structure:* Ted Bundy, who served as his own defense attorney, was moved to Miami for his trial after he argued the impossibility of finding an impartial jury in northern Florida.

Often, as here, we make clauses subordinate in order to combine two independent clauses.

> ❖ *Clumsy structure:* Burton entered his private receiving chambers. General Pleskov was already there.
>
> ❖ *Improved structure:* When Burton entered his private receiving chambers, General Pleskov was already there to greet him.

We combine sentences to improve the flow as well as for other reasons.

> ❖ *Clumsy structure:* To a large extent, caregiving has always been considered a women's issue. Part of the reason might be availability.
>
> ❖ *Improved structure:* To a large extent, caregiving has always been considered a women's role, perhaps in part due to the supposed greater availability of women for the job.

Here, we've combined the sentences to improve the flow and avoid awkwardness.

> ❖ *Clumsy structure:* Jane, her youngest, lived in the country with her husband and four kids, worked in the family business, and still made Nan's independent life possible. Jane was her caregiver.
>
> ❖ *Improved structure:* Nan's youngest, Jane, lived in the country with her husband and four children, worked in the family business, and still made Nan's independent life possible by being her caregiver.

Here we've combined to make sure readers understand the relationship between the idea of Nan's independent life and the idea of the care given by Jane. Is the sentence now optimal? I don't think so. The structure is improved, but I'd continue drafting if this were my project.

Cut and Streamline Sentences

We all know people who rattle on and on. In fact, the word "rattle" in archaic English (a word deleted from current dictionaries by the baby-faced editors) meant someone who rattled, or prattled on endlessly. As listeners, we don't like this sort of speech, nor do we, as readers, enjoy rattling encoded in a written format.

❖ *Poor sentence structure:* Home base is actually Chicago, but I only have a small place there since I spend more time in various points south than I do at headquarters.

❖ *Improved sentence:* My home base is actually Chicago, but I only have a small place there. Most of my time is spent traveling in the South, which is my sales territory.

The first sentence has two independent clauses and two dependent clauses—that's a whole snake's nest of clauses. Let's allow the reader a pause for breath and a moment to catch up and digest the words.

Sometimes we simply eliminate words, rather than cut a sentence in two.

❖ *Too busy:* The last few kids trickled into the overheated band room before the late bell was muffled by the dense air and the stray sounds of saxophones and trumpets setting up.

❖ *Less busy:* The last few kids made it into the overheated band room before the ringing of the late bell was swallowed by the sound of saxophones and trumpets tuning up.

Part of the change you'll note is the toning down of the verb, "trickled," a lovely word, but one that adds to the "noise" of the sentence.

My friend emailed me the following sentence from the nation's newspaper of record and said, "I had to reread it twice because I thought the writer had left something out!"

> ❖ *Squeaking by:* Investigators say that Mr. Rader, who will turn sixty on Wednesday, almost certainly in the solitary jail cell where he has been held since he was charged last week with ten counts of murder, is one of the nation's most notorious and elusive serial killers, the strangler who toyed with Wichita for three decades in letters and poems and packages and who long ago insisted that the public call him B.T.K., for his preferred method: bind, torture, kill.
>
> ❖ *Less breathtaking:* Mr. Rader, alleged to be the B.T.K. (bind, torture, kill) serial strangler, who turns sixty on Wednesday, has been held in solitary confinement since he was charged last Tuesday on ten counts of murder. The notorious B.T.K. eluded Wichita police for three decades while taunting the public with letters, poems, and packages that announced his horrific treatment of victims.

A certain poetry has been lost, perhaps, in making the original more readable, but nineteen words have been saved. For newspaper style, readability and saving space should take precedence over poetry. (Where's a copy editor when you really need one?)

Fragments

To have a complete sentence, we must have a subject and predicate. The subject is a noun or pronoun and the predicate includes a verb that refers to the subject. Generally speaking we don't want to create fragments, which would lack either the subject or the verb. Sometimes a fragment can be used, but rarely, and only with a good purpose in mind.

By the way, an imperative sentence, such as "Go to the office," is not a fragment, though the format seems to be missing a subject. In an imperative sentence, the subject "you" is understood.

> ❖ *Fragment:* And, as we give ourselves the right to look for what we need, and release what is holding us back,

we begin the final stages of our mid-life crisis. The stage where we are willing to move into a future that looks very different from our past.

❖ *Fragment repaired:* And, as we give ourselves the right to look for what we need and release what is holding us back, we begin the final stage of our mid-life crisis, a period during which we are willing to move into a future that looks very different from our past.

Most often a fragment is created by disconnecting a part of a sentence that belongs to the full structure. In the above example, in order to repair the fragment we simply connect the parts of the sentence that go together naturally. Note that I changed "stages" to "stage" because "during which" might make us ask "during which one?" if we say "stages."

A similar type of fragment is created by the use of a dependent clause as if it were an independent clause.

❖ *Dependent clause as a fragment:* John wasn't chosen for the ad. Although he was the more attractive of the two men.

❖ *Complete sentence:* John wasn't chosen for the ad, although he was the more attractive of the two men.

❖ *Complete sentence:* John, the more attractive of the two men, wasn't chosen for the ad.

And, yes, sometimes fragments work just fine.

❖ *Acceptable fragment:* The new commanding officer of the academy entered the room. A woman! How in

> heavens' name had this travesty occurred? A woman!
> Michaels was going to hand in his resignation.
>
> ❖ *Acceptable fragment:* Jerry said he'd be happy to help
>   with the project. Yeah, like sure.

These fragments express brief thoughts effectively. The writer understands she has written a fragment and intends the fragment as a stylistic device.

Comma Splices

While we're discussing the bad habit of simply letting a sentence run on, let's look at the comma splice. The comma splice can be defined as a way of splicing one independent clause onto another, using only a comma. This is not a legitimate means of connecting clauses.

> ❖ *Comma splice:* Joe's appearance hadn't changed much in
>   the past fifteen years, except for a few gray hairs and
>   some laugh lines around his eyes, he still looked like the
>   bat boy he had been.
>
> ❖ *Correct form:* Joe's appearance hadn't changed much in
>   the past fifteen years. Except for a few gray hairs and
>   some laugh lines around his eyes, he still looked like the
>   bat boy he had been.

This one is tricky in that a correct form could also be, "Joe's appearance hadn't changed much in the past fifteen years, except for a few gray hairs and some laugh lines around his eyes." However, this form would require a little editing: "Joe's appearance hadn't changed much in the past fifteen years, except for the addition of a few gray hairs and some laugh lines around his eyes." Yes, we know that the gray and the lines were added, but for the sake of having a clear, logical sentence, let's include the explicit statement.

❖ *Comma splice:* Nancy bought the video from the discount store, she gave it to Jim for his birthday.

❖ *Correct form:* Nancy bought the video from the discount store, and she gave it to Jim for his birthday.

❖ *Correct form:* Nancy bought the video from the discount store, after which she gave it to Jim for his birthday.

❖ *Correct form:* Nancy bought the video she gave Jim for his birthday at a discount store.

To have a correct sentence structure, you can use a coordinating conjunction after the comma to form these two joined, independent (standalone) clauses, or you can create a dependent clause with subordinating conjunctions. Or you can simply integrate the sentence.

Another choice is to split the sentence into two with a period and capital. Though the resulting sentences don't flow well here, sometimes they do: "Nancy bought the video from the discount store. She gave it to Jim for his birthday."

A final choice would be to separate the clauses with a semicolon: "Nancy bought the video from the discount store; she gave it to Jim for his birthday."

Even though this final choice is legitimate, the relationship of the two clauses doesn't actually suggest the use of a semicolon.

Quiz
1. What's a comma splice, and is that a good thing?
2. What's a fragment? Can we ever use one? How do we know?
3. Name three reasons for combining sentences.
4. Name three reasons for cutting sentences into two or more independent sentences or for streamlining a sentence.
5. What three techniques might we use to combine sentences?
6. What three techniques might we use to separate clauses and

form independent sentences?
7. Is poetical phrasing important to the journalist?

Exercise

Can you improve the following paragraphs?

I. Robert picked up his sweater and notebook. He headed for the door. Then he carefully locked the door before going to the curb. He waited for the bus. The bus was battered and usually mud-splattered. It might or might not come this way ever again.

II. If, traditionally, clinical trials at nursing homes have been few and far between, the tide may be turning since, just as Willie Sutton robbed banks because "that's where the money is," researchers are entering long term care facilities because that's where the frail elderly are, and soon, the nursing homes, their residents, and future residents may well be the beneficiaries of new knowledge.

III. Literary critics rant that chick lit shouldn't be *allowed* in print. Chick lit writers fear that the genre has peaked. But, anyway, this trendy offshoot of romance is alive and well. Go into any local bookstores and see the pink cover art. In fact, nearly every sector of popular fiction hopes to institute its own particular version of chick lit.

IV. In a telephone interview with *Today's Medical Report,* Larry Diller, M.D., Walnut Creek, CA, author of *Running on Ritalin* and *Should I Medicate My Child?*, said that he has been prescribing psychostimulants for twenty-seven years. He said that while they are safe, some few children build up a tolerance, these children require higher doses for the same effect, although what disturbs Dr. Diller is that in the last few years children have come to explain their problems in what he called "the language of incompetency and disease."

Answers

Quiz

1. What's a comma splice, and is that a good thing?
    A bad thing, a comma splice is the joining of two independent

clauses with only a comma and no coordinating conjunction.

2. What's a fragment? Can we ever use one? How do we know?

    A fragment is an incomplete sentence, a phrase that doesn't include both a subject and predicate (a predicate being at least a verb) or a dependent clause. We can use fragments in some situations, particularly when the fragment expresses a complete idea.

3. Name three reasons for combining sentences.

    We might combine sentences to avoid having several short, choppy sentences; to otherwise improve the flow of a sentence; to show how ideas relate to one another; to avoid using a repeated or stagnant subject; or to avoid using a repeated or uninteresting verb.

4. Name three reasons for cutting sentences into two or more independent sentences or for streamlining a sentence.

    We might cut a sentence into two or more sentences or streamline the sentence if the typical reader might be unable to easily follow the sentence as is; if we have too many clauses for the single sentence structure; or simply to allow the reader to catch his mental breath.

5. What three techniques might we use to combine sentences?

    We might combine sentences by creating a subordinate clause from one of the independent clauses presented as sentences; by eliminating a useless subject and verb; by rearranging the clauses and phrases; and/or by dropping redundant or unnecessary information from one or both of the sentences being combined.

6. What three techniques might we use to separate clauses and form independent sentences?

    We might remove a subordinating element from a dependent clause. We might simply put in a period capital. We might add an interesting subject and/or verb.

7. Is poetical phrasing important to the journalist?

    The journalist strives always to write eloquently, although this approach is most appropriate for features and reviews. For the news story, readability and efficient word use are more important than a flashy style.

Exercise

Suggested Paragraph Improvements:

I. Robert picked up his sweater and notebook and headed for the door, which he carefully locked before going to the curb. Here he waited for a battered and usually mud-splattered yellow school bus that might or might not come this way ever again.

II. If, traditionally, clinical trials at nursing homes have been few and far between, the tide may be turning. Just as Willie Sutton robbed banks because "that's where the money is," researchers are entering long term care facilities since that's where the frail elderly are. Soon, the nursing homes, their residents, and future residents may well be the beneficiaries of resulting new knowledge.

III. Despite periodic rants from literary critics that chick lit shouldn't be *allowed* in print and fearful speculation from chick lit writers that the genre has peaked, this trendy offshoot of romance is alive and well and filling local bookstores with pink cover art. In fact, the form has prospered so enormously that nearly every sector of popular fiction hopes to institute its own particular version.

IV. In a telephone interview with *Today's Medical Report,* Larry Diller, M.D., Walnut Creek, CA, author of *Running on Ritalin* and *Should I Medicate My Child?*, said that he has been prescribing psychostimulants for twenty-seven years, and that while they are safe, some few children build up a tolerance and require higher doses for the same effect. What disturbs Dr. Diller is that in the last few years children have come to explain their problems in words he called "the language of incompetency and disease."

A Penny a Word—You Pay

GMH: *What common style mistake bugs you the most?*
Phyllis Grann, vice-chair, Random House, New York: *The use of unnecessary words.*

Writers being paid by the word say that instead of "bang," they might write "bang, bang, bang" for gunshots. That's really a joke—sort of. While often the length of a story or article is fixed by guidelines, and a flat fee is paid, sometimes writers do get paid by the word, even today. But any writer imagining that adding unnecessary words to a piece is a good idea isn't the writer who is going to sell the story or the article. And that's the long way of saying the best writing is economical writing. How many words should the story or article be? As many as telling the story takes, but not a single word more.

Instead of being paid a penny a word, five cents a word, or a dollar a word—and all these are legitimate current pay scales, to be sure—imagine that *you* will have to pay for every word you put on the page. Use what you need, but be a little bit frugal in your word use. Like every good householder or starving artist, consider your budget.

Keep in mind, too, that most publishers aren't looking for a first book that runs one-hundred-and-sixty-thousand words, because they have to account for printing costs, paper prices, and the storage charge for maintaining inventory in a warehouse somewhere. Thus the words allotted a just-hatched author won't be unlimited.

And if you're seeking to market pieces to a magazine or newspaper, start on the abbreviated side in that realm as well. Try placing a letter to the editor, then sell small fillers until the editors know your name and see that you have some command of the language along with a few ideas worth setting into type.

As for your short story lengths, make your short fiction reasonably short. An editor trying to fill a magazine with a variety of pieces for an issue isn't really likely to buy a ten-thousand-word story— again, especially from an author whose name isn't a draw. So when counting words in a work, less may actually be more, but, really, use all the words that you need in order to write the piece optimally. As a matter of style, though, ditch the words not required to express the ideas, and be properly clear and rhythmical while you're at it.

Here are some examples:

> ❖ *Extra words:* But I wanted to get an idea of the lay of the land.
>
> ❖ *Trimmed:* But I wanted to understand the lay of the land.

As you write, as well as when you edit your own writing, you need to stay alert for words that aren't required and to cull them. This is still another automatic mental habit you want to form as a writer.

> ❖ *Extra words:* "We are waiting for only two more people at our table, so why don't you have a seat?"
>
> ❖ *Trimmed:* "We're waiting for only two more, so please join us."

Express the idea. And when writing fiction, express the idea as the character would. But rarely will you need to go on at great length.

> ❖ *Extra words:* His headlights reflecting off the wet pavement made it difficult to spot all the potholes, and

> his unmarked department vehicle bounced uncomfortably along.
>
> ❖ *Trimmed:* His unmarked vehicle bounced along the wet blacktop, making him curse.

One thing we want to think about when writing is how much description a bit of business actually deserves. How important, for instance, is the setting? How important are the details? If the setting and details aren't important, then don't include a lot of extras. We're living in an age of impatient readers. Cut back on description; sketch in background material.

On the other hand, you might want to include very specific details, such as the name of a street or an area of the city, even the make of the car. Details help to fill in the picture and to add color, while not actually taking that many words. Do we think the writer who created the above knows Detroit? No. Specific details will make our readers trust us more.

Pithy but with detail: His unmarked DPD vehicle bounced over the wet blacktop alongside Kronk Recreation Center, making him curse.

Where's the Beef ?

In addition to our being efficient in wording, let's try packing both our articles and our fiction with interesting information. If you don't have that, even in fiction, you don't have anything. You have air. If you give us only air (a lot of nothing), at least give us blank pages where we can rest our eyes. Don't bother us with the dinning nuisance of more words in an overly wordy universe.

> ❖ *Too gabby: I'm Finally Out of School—Now What?* is designed to provide down-to-earth, helpful advice as you begin this next phase of your life. Many of the subjects we'll cover are things most people out in the world take for granted, but you might not yet have encountered the reality of needing to deal with such everyday circumstances.

Claim your free access to www.firstwriter.com: See p.263

> ❖ *Cut to the chase: I'm Finally Out of School—Now What?* will cover many aspects of everyday life that people living on their own for the first time should understand.

By the way, neither Mies van der Rohe nor Buckminster Fuller originally said "less is more," although both used the philosophy as an approach to design. Robert Browning coined the line in his 1855 poem, *Andrea del Sarto*, about the real-life painter (1486-1531). In writing as well as architecture and the visual arts, less can certainly be more. Implication will often trump the more overt. Suggestion can have more power than lengthy and explicit detail. Of course, we might add here, "but that depends," because we also need a certain amount of specificity and explication.

Don't Equivocate

The best writing is forceful and direct, but often writers are so eager to pinpoint an exact concept—ninety percent of this, but ten percent of that—that they water down the sentence by equivocating.

> ❖ *Wishy washy:* He had seemingly disappeared into thin air.
>
> ❖ *Direct:* He had disappeared into thin air.

The reader knows he didn't actually disappear into thin air, but that something untoward probably happened to him. Yes, I just equivocated by the use of the word "probably," and that's because he might have engineered his own disappearance. I'm not entirely against equivocation, you see, but I want to bring the consideration to mind.

Often we use extra words to waffle on one point or another. We might ask ourselves if we really should introduce that wiggle room for a statement, diminishing the strength of the idea and the sentence itself.

That's it for the chapter, folks.

Exercise

Improve upon the following, if possible (it is).

1. Previously, when early music was performed, it was blown up into big, beefy 19th-century big-orchestra arrangements or consigned to the holiday ghetto of Messiah and revels merrymaking.
2. Musicians and musicologists in the 1960s and since have been finding treasures in scores that had been crumbling in various local libraries for hundreds of years.
3. Jane believes life has no new challenges and she's doomed to middle-aged ennui. She is a romance novelist, mother, and wife.
4. His miracle wheat technology then became the catalyst that fomented the "green revolution" that averted famine in India and Pakistan by the late 1960s.
5. However, there will be times when you will find it hard to interpret a symbol in the context of your query.
6. She was dressed in a white cotton sleeping gown, her long, silvery-white hair braided and resting beside her on the pillow, which cradled her head.
7. It will help them understand the issues and nudge them to begin to prepare to avoid these matters becoming problems in their own lives.
8. The words spilled out of his mouth, gathering as if he couldn't stop them and perhaps he couldn't.
9. For this work he was awarded the Nobel Peace Prize in 1970. That was just the start of the next phase of his career.
10. This book was written for children but it appeals to adults as well, I think, because it has all the elements of a good story: a likeable protagonist and despicable antagonists, but also surprises and a good mystery element as well.

Suggested changes:

1. Previously, when early music was performed, it was blown up into big, beefy 19th-century big-orchestra arrangements or consigned to the holiday ghetto of Messiah and revels merrymaking.
   Previously, early music in performance was blown up into beefy 19thcentury big-orchestra arrangements or consigned

to the holiday ghetto of Messiah or revels merrymaking.

2. Musicians and musicologists in the 1960s and since have been finding treasures in scores that had been crumbling in various local libraries for hundreds of years.

   Musicologists since the 1960s have been finding treasures in scores crumbling for a hundred years or more in local libraries.

3. Jane believes life has no new challenges and she's doomed to middle-aged ennui. She is a romance novelist, mother, and wife.

   Jane, romance novelist, mother, and wife, believes life has no new challenges, dooming her to middle-aged ennui.

4. His miracle wheat technology then became the catalyst that fomented the "green revolution" that averted famine in India and Pakistan by the late 1960s.

   His miracle wheat technology became the force behind the "green revolution" that averted famine in India and Pakistan during the 1960s.

5. However, there will be times when you will find it hard to interpret a symbol in the context of your query.

   However, at times you will have difficulty interpreting a symbol in the context of your query.

6. She was dressed in a white cotton sleeping gown, her long. silvery-white hair braided and resting beside her on the pillow, which cradled her head.

   She was dressed in a white cotton sleeping gown, her long, silvery hair braided and resting beside her on the pillow.

7. It will help them understand the issues and nudge them to begin to prepare to avoid these matters becoming problems in their own lives.

   It will help them understand the issues and nudge them to avoid similar problems in their own lives.

8. The words spilled out of his mouth, gathering as if he couldn't stop them and perhaps he couldn't.

   The words spilled out of his mouth as if he couldn't stop them, and perhaps he couldn't.

9. For this work he was awarded the Nobel Peace Prize in 1970. That was just the start of the next phase of his career.

   For this work he received the Nobel Peace Prize in 1970,

which started the next phase of his career.

10. This book was written for children but it appeals to adults as well, I think, because it has all the elements of a good story: a likeable protagonist and despicable antagonists, but also surprises and a good mystery element as well.

This book, written for children, appeals to adults, too, because it has all the elements of a good story: a likeable protagonist, despicable antagonists, surprises along the way, and a strong mystery element. (What does "good" mean?)

Writing Pros Look at Style

There is no royal path to good writing; and such paths as exist do not lead through neat critical gardens, various as they are, but through the jungles of self, the world, and of craft.

—Jessamyn West

I interviewed a bunch of writers for this section. A couple of them thought that by "grammar" I meant Grandma, and theirs had died. One woman offered to edit this book, but she had a comma splice in her note to me and used a plural pronoun with a singular antecedent. Finally, I decided to use only two pieces, those by women whose names begin with a "K." Ultra-selective, maybe, but... <shrug>.

Kit Sloane

Kit, who served as an editor at *Futures* magazine for a time, was traveling the country (and Cambridge, England) promoting *Extreme Cuisine*, her latest in the Margot O'Banion & Max Skull Mystery Series, when I caught up with her. I've known Kit since she edited at *Futures*, but our conversation about Grandma (oh, see, I keep making that mistake myself) and style took place just as we were about to meet person to person for the first time at a writing conference.

GMH: How important is having a "correct" or appropriate writing style?

KS: Poor grammar or poor word usage turns me off in the books I read and I certainly don't want to subject my readers to these errors, especially when, with a little work, they are easily remedied. I enjoy pushing the stylistic envelope a bit, though, when it fits. For instance, in a novel I just wrote, I put a scene in screenplay style.

My choice works at that spot because the scene takes place on a movie set.

GMH: Do you try to improve in areas of composition?

KS: I keep several stylebooks next to my desk. I also query editor friends if I'm really in the dark about something specific. I think writers seek to improve the quality of their writing every time they revise. If they aren't trying to make it better, why are they revising in the first place?

GMH: When you were the editor at *Futures*, what type of style goofs did you see most often? Would these mean a rejection?

KS: I encountered a lot of poor grammar as well as misused and misspelled words. These problems prompted quick rejection. I don't think it's fair for a writer to expect an editor to slog through glitches like those in order to get to the "brilliant" story. I like clean copy and writing that enhances the story, not poor construction that detracts.

GMH: What is your pet peeve in terms of writing style and how might this be corrected?

KS: I very much dislike misuse of commas. Of course, I'm as guilty of this as anyone, although I do have books dog-eared on the "how to punctuate with commas" portions. I wish all the rules were hard and fast. But, as in most creative endeavors, some rules are loose and writers must make decisions based on the best input they can find.

Kristine Kathryn Rusch

Former editor of the prestigious *The Magazine of Fantasy and Science Fiction*, Kristine Kathryn Rusch has won awards in mystery, romance, science fiction, and fantasy. Her novels have made various bestseller lists and have been published in fourteen countries and thirteen different languages. Currently, she is writing a series in each of her genres: the Retrieval Artist series in science fiction; the Smokey Dalton series in mystery (written as Kris Nelscott); the Fates series in romance (written as Kristine

Grayson); and the upcoming Fantasy Life series in fantasy.

GMH: How important is having an appropriate writing style to being published?

KKR: First, you *must* know grammar and spelling before you can even develop a personal style. But correct grammar and spelling are not a style. In fact, once you learn all the rules, in fiction at least, you must forget them. This is where workshops do the most harm to writers. Workshops insist on perfect grammar, believing it is style. In fiction, style is a good voice, which often requires broken rules. If you don't believe me, type a sample paragraph from Joyce Carol Oates, James Lee Burke, Stephen King, and Larry McMurtry into your computer, and then run the grammar checker. It'll scream at you.

GMH: Have you always been stylistically correct or did you have to learn various aspects of style? Do you keep on trying to improve in areas of style?

KKR: Sadly, I learned grammar in my nine years of studying Spanish. Until then, I didn't have a clue about past participle and future tense. Fortunately, I come from a literate family who insisted on good grammar. I also read and read and read and read, so grammar became ingrained. I work on style all the time. I actively study other writers (after I've read their stories as a reader—for pure enjoyment—to get what they're trying to do). Sometimes I even stop and type a sentence into my own computer, trying to figure out what the writer did. I've learned a lot from other writers. I mentioned Stephen King. He has a way of manipulating time that is just brilliant. He does it all through punctuation and tense.

GMH: When you edited *F&SF* what kind of style errors did you most commonly find? Did you reject on the basis of style errors?

KKR: I always insisted on a cover letter. A cover letter is a great test. If the writer made three or more spelling errors or grammatical errors in the cover letter, then I assumed that the grammatical errors in the manuscript were not on purpose. If the cover letter was in good shape, but the errors in the writing were random and made no sense, then I would reject as quickly as possible. If the errors had a point—the character is mentally challenged, for example (think

William Faulkner's *The Sound and the Fury*)—then I kept reading until the writer threw me out by character details, illogic, or bad story-telling.

GMH: What is your pet peeve in terms of writing style and how might this be corrected?

KKR: I have no problems with the pros. They do what they do. If I don't like their voice, then that's personal taste. I have many pet peeves with the near-pros and English teachers who insist on correct grammar and call that style. My peeves are that they are destroying a lot of original voices by forcing them to conform. Fiction is about breaking the rules. Of course, you must learn the rules before you break them. This is not an excuse to skip this area of craft. You must be the very, very best you can be at everything in writing—from use of commas to use of setting.

PART IV

Mechanics, AKA Punctuation

The Fine Art of Reading

If you can see the sense of punctuation—
Those dots, and lines, and squiggles on the page;
You'll master any language situation,
And be applauded as a punctuation sage.
        —Marie Rackham, punctuation sage

An important key to being able to write, especially to punctuating correctly, is being able to read properly. Unfortunately, most people don't read in the right way, with the exact nuance of the punctuation, the correct pause. As with most developmental benchmarks, if you miss this one, you must work doubly hard to cue your nervous system to the signals and responses that should have been incorporated into your sensory tool belt earlier on. All is not lost, however. Anyone driven enough who has a problem in this area can train herself and learn the language of reading word for word, punctuation mark for punctuation mark.

To begin with, you will want to read material out loud. When you read out loud, you're less likely to skip over a word or the punctuation and less likely to fool yourself about how something sounds. Bear in mind that every word, every comma and semicolon affects the rhythm of the whole. That's why we want to be sure to leave nothing out when we read.

In this segment, I'll discuss punctuation and such in relationship to reading, not to the rules. The rules are a different consideration, and I go over those in another chapter. Remember: How you read, that is, your ear, isn't going to be the definitive arbiter as to where the comma goes. Rules rule. Go by the rules. But if your ear is good, you will begin to understand where punctuation might go, and you'll seek verification in the rules, or even try to wing it now and again <wink>. No, no, check the rules.

Claim your free access to **www.firstwriter.com**: See p.263

Commas

Reading a comma requires a slight pause, just a flicker, just enough to give us a quarter beat of rest. The comma slows down the words so the reader can consider them better and not run over any on the way to the period. The comma also allows the reader to mentally organize the words into groups that form patterns of meaning. Commas are very important because of their contribution to this structuring of "significance." The comma is the most frequently used punctuation mark.

Semicolons

Semicolons create a longer pause between elements than a comma, but a shorter pause than a full stop—the period. The better writers use this mark fairly rarely in separating independent clauses, because the conditions for the semicolon's necessary use (as opposed to the *why-don't-I-stick-one-in—they're-fancy* use) actually arise quite infrequently. We use the semicolon to join/separate two independent clauses when the clauses are very intimately tied, and the meaning of the second clause "hangs on" the information in the first. If you can use a "period capital" instead of a semicolon and not detect much difference in the meaning, then use the period capital.

The thing about the semicolon's effect on the reader is that, because it's rare, several on a page can attract some notice. A single use now and again won't really raise even a solitary hair on an eyebrow, but when the mark begins to intrude its presence on the page with some frequency, the reader becomes distracted by the mark. One nun in traditional garb (God bless her) won't draw a great deal of interest in a crowd, but send a number of them walking through, here and there, and the average observer begins to pay attention and to wonder.

Periods

Periods, of course, create a full stop when used with a sentence or a fragment. That's the beat against which all the other pauses are measured. The period is the signal that the sentence or fragment has come to an end. Yet, oddly, its use elsewhere doesn't actually accomplish the same result. In saying "Mr. Fowler" or "the U.N. headquarters," we don't slow down. Have I mentioned lately how counterintuitive the language is? Why, then, do we use a period? It's an enigma.

Exclamation Points!

The exclamation point should be used minimally. The reason? The exclamation point at the end of a word or the end of a sentence is like a hammer coming down on wood. Bang! How many times do you need that in a work? Certainly not three times a paragraph or even on a page. Some new writers use the exclamation point quite a lot, and the effect on the editor or agent— this piece never gets to the end user, an actual reader, mind you, due to the excessive exclamations—is of a breathless teenager trying to get across a point he's excited about.

Any repeated inflection in speech or in writing begins to grate on the nerves. That's especially true of the exclamation mark. If you really, really need the mark, use it. But consider allowing the words themselves to carry the message of excitement, remarkableness, or urgency.

When you're reading out loud and want to show the exclamation point, you'll give a lot of emphasis to the sentence and, especially, to the sentence finish. If you discover this is overdone for your own taste, then you may well imagine that the reader will find the exclamations a bit excessive as well.

Hyphens

Hyphens, also, are an important structuring device and present sort of the opposite of the comma's pause, since they pull words together, perhaps a tenth of a beat. (The timings I describe are subjective.) But remember, hyphens, too, present a visual signal that when used profusely can attract too much notice. Hyphens are one of the least certain of the punctuation marks, and the current style is to reduce their use. Still, the hyphen is of value in arranging words in idea patterns.

Capitals

Capitals do read differently than lower case, which is why if we write in all capitals on the Internet, people think we're shouting. Capitalizing a word produces an emphasis, a louder resonance. We might want that, but, then again, we might not. If we don't know when a capital is legitimately used, our use of one in the wrong place will make the writing seem as if we're drawing a bit of attention to the word or words in an odd way.

We sometimes use an outdated or peculiar capital deliberately in fiction in a period piece or in a science fiction story. For instance: "William Pitt had been recalled by his King in 1804" might work in an historical novel. If we were writing this in nonfiction, however, we would have to say, "William Pitt had been recalled by his king in 1804," because we don't capitalize job titles and "king" is simply a job title.

I had an Irish student who capitalized almost every Noun she wrote. Apparently when she had been growing up, that was how the Teachers taught her to write. Perhaps the Teachers were Nuns or perhaps they were under the Influence of the Germans, as the Irish and Germans were cozy during the War. German Nouns, of course, are capitalized. (Well, that explains that—not.) At any rate, if you don't want a stilted emphasis on certain words, try for appropriate capitalization. Inappropriate capitals aren't a mere nothing, in other words; they change the way the sentence is read.

> ❖ *Too hyper-sounding:* I hope you'll find time to enjoy the beauty of our Massachusetts countryside without worrying about your Grade Point Averages.
>
> ❖ *More normal:* I hope you'll find time to enjoy the beauty of our Massachusetts countryside without worrying about your grade point averages.

Question Marks

When we ask a question and when we read a sentence with a question mark, we raise our inflection at the end. That's how a question sounds when we speak the English language and how we read a question with a question mark. We don't do that when we read a rhetorical question that ends with a question mark, however: "Will you cut that out?" Even with the question mark, such a sentence is read more as a statement (but with a dash of question and a speckle of exclamation).

Apostrophes

The apostrophe doesn't itself have a sound. The only consideration when reading or writing material with apostrophes is how possessives sound and whether or not to use an additional "s" after an apostrophe when a word ends with an "s."

❖ *Correct:* That car was Les'. He borrowed James' car last week.

❖ *Correct:* That car was Les's. He borrowed James's car last week.

Although we may choose the first version, the second version allows the additional "s" to clearly signal that a possessive has been stated. True that our eyes see the apostrophe with the first set and we know that we have possessives here, but we haven't also signaled our inner ear. The second version is more useful for the reader.

Colons

The colon creates a pause a smidgeon longer than the pause created by a semicolon. Just a smidge, mind you.

❖ *Correct:* I filled my dance card; I'll dance with John, Henry, Ralph, and Ed.

❖ *Correct:* I filled my dance card: I'll dance with John, Henry, Ralph, and Ed.

I've tried it a few times. The colon creates a tad bit more of a stop. The interruption is slightly greater than with the semicolon.

Parentheses and Brackets

Parentheses present material in a quiet way. The words are taken out of the sentence, in a sense, and encapsulated. Thus the effect is of someone speaking in a subdued voice. The information may be important, but it's certainly not shouted. Brackets, because they are used infrequently and mostly as a kind of academic option, bury the material they enclose even a bit further. That doesn't mean the material is ignored, because the added bits may be quite consequential. But brackets don't make the writing shine—so don't expect them to; however, using brackets will make you seem awfully intelligent. (Not kidding.)

Dashes

Dashes don't "remove" the material, dimming the sound, in the same way that parentheses do. I once (upon a time) used a million parentheses—whereas now I use only one hundred thousand—while I staff the rest of my asides with the bold and daring (dashing) dash. The dash does have a little bit of a breathless quality that says "I'm just going to move right along here, regardless of convention," but at the same time, it adds a piece of punctuation allowing the reader to take a bit of a breath so a sentence may keep on going. Long sentences aren't always hard to read because they're too long, but can be difficult because the punctuation doesn't permit a beat or two of rest along the way. A dash can help. The dash or dashes may be used in quite formal writing all the same, even in academic writing. Although, as I mention above, the dash may be dashing, it's dashing in the same way that a well-outfitted British gentleman might be—that is, dashing, but very, very proper.

Quotation Marks

Have a read:

❖ "What are you thinking, honey?" Sue wanted to know.

❖ "Poor sod that spilled the water on me. It's a rotten life. Human beings are really a degenerate bunch, the way we treat one another."

❖ Sue squeezed his arm and beamed at him happily. "Don't worry, Walter's going to take you on," she assured him, not exactly a non-sequitur, since she could read his mind.

❖ What was he thinking, Sue wanted to know.

❖ *Poor sod who'd spilled the water on him,* Jack told her. *What a rotten life. Human beings were really a degenerate bunch, the way they treated one another.*

❖ Sue squeezed his arm, beamed at him happily, and told him not to worry, that Walter was going to take him on—not exactly a non-sequitur, since she could read his mind.

To me, the writing in quote marks seems clear and spoken, not *thought* the way material in unquoted text comes across.

Paragraph Breaks

The sound does change with a paragraph break, even to the extent that we might have to rewrite the sentence that starts the new paragraph. Because, as we're writing along in the old paragraph, we've gotten into a rhythm of continuation that, while not droning or patterned exactly, does have a quality of "forging forth." A break in the paragraph means a longer pause than with the period and much more of a halt. The new paragraph is a new start, entirely, and often we have to remind the reader what we're talking about. Yes, we were just discussing that in the last sentence, as we were when the first sentence of the new paragraph was simply part of the last paragraph. But the longer break, the sense that we have "refreshed" the conversation—something like refreshing a Web page online—means that we've wiped the slate clean. We've made a shift in context, even though the content remains the same. This isn't so much a matter of sound this time, but of feeling.

Italics

Italic definitely "sounds" different than Roman type. Read the following paragraphs:

❖ Filing over the crosswalk, which was walled with picture windows, they peered down at the most stupendous view Jack had ever seen in this picturesque town. A brilliant sun, that staggering flamethrower of his childhood, seared over a landscape of three bodies of water viewed at once. The Bay of Biscayne, the Atlantic Ocean, and the canal on which the hospital sat were each shaded distinctly.

❖ *Filing over the crosswalk, which was walled with picture windows, they peered down at the most stupendous view Jack had ever seen in this picturesque town. A brilliant sun, that staggering flamethrower of his childhood, seared over a landscape of three bodies of water viewed at once. The Bay of Biscayne, the Atlantic Ocean, and the canal on which the hospital sat were each shaded distinctly.*

Do these two version read the same in your head? They shouldn't. The italic removes a little of the immediacy from the writing. The writing becomes more of a whisper in a fog, more dreamlike, the sound more wrapped in cotton wool. The italic also becomes a bit annoying to read.

Picking Punctuation
Understanding what punctuation marks do can help you decide how to punctuate.

❖ *Hard to read:* I was drawn to the building by the arches. The two story tan brick and white stucco building reminded me of the old Spanish style homes scattered throughout South Florida.

❖ *Better:* I was drawn to the building by the arches. The two-story, tan brick and white stucco building reminded me of the old Spanish-style homes scattered throughout South Florida.

I inserted a comma after "two-story," because with so many adjectives jumping out at us, the quarter pause makes the reading easier. The hyphens also help to organize the many words demanding attention.

❖ *Good:* The pool, he'd told his son, was the thumbprint of God, filled with celestial tears shed in mourning for what His people had done to the land. Dominick had left the world of organized religion, returned and left again, all the while searching for a God he could feel in his heart, a God requiring no sanctification by self-appointed holy men.

❖ *Better:* The pool, he'd told his son, was the thumbprint of God, filled with celestial tears shed in mourning for what His people had done to the land.

Dominick had left the world of organized religion, returned and left again, all the while searching for a God he could feel in his heart, a God requiring no sanctification by self-appointed holy men.

When we break the paragraph, we allow the last sentence in the prior paragraph to linger a moment and not be lost. We also emphasize the first sentence in the next paragraph. Of course, here, we obviously have a shift in topic from paragraph one to paragraph two and so really have to break the paragraph, anyway.

❖ *Good:* Nathan fell backward as his feet left the rail car platform and flew up into the air. He flipped over into a jumble of men all tangled up elbow to eye socket.

❖ *Better:* Nathan fell backward as his feet left the rail car platform and flew up into the air. He flipped over into a jumble of men all tangled up, elbow to eye socket.

This is a fairly complex set of actions; the added comma is the least we can do for it. The comma, in emphasizing the "elbow to eye socket," also adds to the humor.

The only exercise for this chapter is to become aware of how punctuation sounds, if you aren't already. The rest of this section of the book will give you the rules. Once you read over the rules, you'll have a much better idea of how to punctuate. Keep thinking in terms of how the writing *sounds*, because the more sophisticated readers *are* listening.

"Speak the Speech As I Pronounced It to You," Said Hamlet

I am big! It's the pictures that got small."
—Sunset Boulevard

"Play it, Sam. Play 'As Time Goes By.' "
—Casablanca

"You know how to whistle, don't you, Steve? You just put your lips together and blow."
—To Have and Have Not

Speech, that is, dialogue in fiction, or quotes in nonfiction, must be cited in a particular way. This is a very basic format that we see nearly every time we read a book or periodical—which is why a writer's getting this small number of specific conventions so very wrong is somewhat puzzling. Although not much in writing dialogue can go awry, every aspect of dialogue or quotes that can be written incorrectly, often is.

Commas for Quotes

❖ *Correct:* "Speak the speech, I pray you, as I pronounced it to you," said Hamlet.

That's a model format for dialogue or quotes. We use a comma inside the quote marks (which is what we always do in the United

States of America these days), and we use a word of citation with that. Words of citation attribute spoken words to the person uttering them: *said, told* (with an object, as in "told her"), *repeated, added, noted, commented, remarked, explained, continued, refuted, stuttered, yelled, countered, sputtered,* and so on.

❖ *Incorrect:* "I love him." The duchess confided.

❖ *Incorrect:* "I love him," The duchess confided.

❖ *Correct:* "I love him," the duchess confided.

Let me note here that a word processor's auto format feature may lead to errors if we aren't careful. With quoted speech, if we make a typo and use a period instead of a comma inside the quote, we will get what we see as the first incorrect sentence above: "I love him." The duchess confided. In this case, the auto formatting of MS Word gave us the capital "T" after the period. The writer who doesn't read over his work will appear ignorant as to the proper punctuation with quotes.

Without words of citation, we don't use a comma.

❖ *Incorrect:* "I love him," the duchess lifted her glass.

❖ *Correct:* "I love him." The duchess lifted her glass.

Generally speaking, we use a capital with the first word in a quote of a full sentence or more. If the sentence is interrupted and a further quote continues the sentence, the second bit is not capitalized (we're in the middle of the sentence, for goodness sake).

❖ *Incorrect:* The secretary of state said, "we are hopeful that we can resolve this situation quickly."

❖ *Correct:* Secretary of State Colin Powell said, "We are hopeful that we can resolve this situation quickly."

❖ *Incorrect:* "We are hopeful," the secretary of state said, "That we can resolve this situation quickly."

❖ *Correct:* "We are hopeful," the secretary of state said, "that we can resolve this situation quickly."

Although the second part of a sentence isn't capitalized in a continuing quote, this is something I see students do all the time.

Also note when we do and when we don't capitalize titles such as "secretary of state." We capitalize a title when it's used as part of a name or in place of a name—only.

❖ *Incorrect:* The road to peace is "Pretty slippery," said the secretary of state.

❖ *Correct:* The road to peace is "pretty slippery," said Secretary of State Colin Powell.

I actually don't know if Secretary of State Colin Powell said any such thing, but I want to reinforce the difference in the title use. Obviously a fragment is not capitalized in the way a full sentence is.

When we cite speech but use a "that," a special rule applies, and we don't capitalize even if the quote seems to be a full sentence. We also don't use a comma, even though we use a verb of citation.

❖ *Incorrect:* The finance minister commented that "The exchange ratio has been very weak."

❖ *Correct:* The finance minister commented that "the exchange ratio has been very weak."

I would say the "that" actually makes the quoted portion a dependent clause rather than a full sentence, which is why the capital is obviated, but regardless of the explanation, this is the rule. Sometimes when we use a "that," we can simply eliminate the quote marks and quote indirectly if the quote seems too clumsy or not particularly interesting as a quote per se. Even if the words are exactly what a subject said, we might want to replace the quote with simple, unquoted narration.

❖ *Quoted with a "that":* Lead author Nick Medford noted that "...interest in depersonalisation [*sic*] disorder can be found in commentary published during the 1920s through the 1940s."

❖ *Without quotes:* Lead author Nick Medford noted that interest in depersonalization disorder can be found in commentary published during the 1920s through the 1940s.

As an aside, the "*sic*," from the Latin, meaning "thus," shows that the original had the word or words as they appear in the quote. In this case, "depersonalisation" is the spelling used in Dr. Medford's article in a British journal, although the spelling we generally use in the U.S. is "depersonalization." Note too that "*sic*" is generally bracketed because it's used primarily in quotes, but can be placed in parentheses outside of quotes. I researched the use of the "*sic*" in all the style guides on which I could lay my hands and decided, in general, to simply use a footnote when material is not in direct quotes. Here, of course, I just changed the spelling of the word to U.S. spelling in the revised version.

We All Sound Like Idiots—Help Us

I'd also like to add about quoting that unless we're writing for a newspaper of record, such as *The New York Times*, amelioration of a person's spoken words is best. I once worked with a writer who reproduced a long conversation exactly as the conversation occurred. I was both amused and appalled. Don't let your interviewee think he sounds like an idiot—or let readers agree. Smooth over the speech.

❖ *Sounding like an idiot:* "Well, we're also going to continue with the prior benchmarks, let's see, pain and the others, they were, uh, pressure ulcers, depression, and unrestrained use of restraints. We're going to continue with those when we sign the new contract for the 8th Scope...and will be under contract for other system improvements. I think the new guidelines will include... Well, we want to make sure the resident can make her own decisions as to when she's in charge of some types of ordinary things such as getting up, meals, and being toileted."

❖ *Repaired quote:* "The work of the 7th Scope, looking at pain, pressure ulcers, depression, and restraints, will continue into the 8th Scope, but in addition to these systems improvements, the QIOs will work to make sure the individual resident is in charge of when she's awakened, when she eats, and when she's toileted." (That's pretty simple and straightforward and not too much to remember.)

Interrupted Speech

Some writers chronically interrupt quoted speech with commentary in the middle of a sentence. This might be okay once in a while, but any pattern can be overkill. This interruption generally leads to incorrect punctuation.

❖ *Interrupted sentence:* "The markets don't inevitably make it back to prior levels," he put on his coat while he continued to harangue, "within the investor's lifetime."

❖ *Corrected sentence:* "The markets don't inevitably make it back to prior levels..." He put on his coat while he continued his harangue. "...within the investor's lifetime."

Other Punctuation With Quotes

Sometimes we add parenthetical information to a quote. We do that in brackets.

> ❖ *Not quite:* Dr. Norman Borlaug "has saved hundreds of millions of people from starvation."
>
> ❖ *Better:* "[Dr. Norman Borlaug] has saved hundreds of millions of people from starvation."

Sometimes we use a colon with quotes. Usually, we use the colon when the material quoted is more than a few sentences, especially if it's from another written work, but sometimes we use a colon for a special purpose.

> ❖ *Colon with quote:* Frankly, I don't want to hear about diaper changing and tales of sudden labor, long or short, or exactly how easily these women conceived: "I swear my husband and I can just be in the same room..." I need to pinch these women.

The colon here is the usual type of colon indicating related material follows.

> ❖ *Colon with quote:* His mother used to tell him: "We're all just entertainment for the stars."

I'd use a colon because this is a pretty lofty kind of quote and not a present time one. Of course, here you could use a comma.

Every Sentence Must End

Another aspect of the quote that many writers also fail to understand is that sentences end within quotes just as they do outside of quotes. I'm being a bit sarcastic, I suppose, and venting. Sorry.

> ❖ *Incorrect comma:* "I didn't send for you," Stalin told the ambassador, "you have no business here."
>
> ❖ *Correct punctuation:* "I didn't send for you," Stalin told the ambassador. "You have no business here."

The quote divides into two sentences, the first accompanied by the attribution that carries through to the second quoted portion. This brings us to the fact that we generally only give a single attribution in a paragraph, but certainly only one to a quote.

> ❖ *Incorrect, double citation:* The OIG spokesman stated further, "Follow-up work is sometimes performed after some of our studies. However, at this point, no determination has been made as to what additional work may be done in this area," White clarified.
>
> ❖ *Correct, single citation:* The OIG spokesman stated further, "Follow-up work is sometimes performed after some of our studies. However, at this point, no determination has been made as to what additional work may be done in this area."

New Paragraph for Each Speaker

Another convention to which we adhere is that we do not put the quoted speech of more than one person in a paragraph. This gives us a visual clue as to who is speaking.

> ❖ *Wrong paragraph format with quotes:* "I looked at the contact sheet in our disaster plan and called the rescue squad," said Robinson. "We then called the families," added Jackson.
>
> ❖ *Correct paragraph format with quotes:* "I looked at the contact sheet in our disaster plan and called the

rescue squad," said Robinson.

"We then called the families," added Jackson.

However, sometimes we may quote several unidentified speakers in one paragraph.

❖ *Correct:* A number of absurd responses issued forth, much to Marsha's distress. "Not me." "Let's all rush the office." "Do or die!"

Such multiple-speaker, quoted speech can also be broken into paragraphs, but the above is obviously a much more efficient approach. Do what you will. In the final analysis, if the material is published, the house style will prevail or the editor/copy editor will make the ultimate decision.

Quotes That Continue

Sometimes quotes continue from one paragraph to the next. We have a formalized convention for punctuating that.

❖ *Wrong format:* "Don't let them do that to you, partner. You have a choice. Blah Blah Blah.
When I want to London in 1989, they told me I had to sign a release, so I did. I since have heard that many of my fellow inductees didn't."

❖ *Correct format:* "Don't let them do that to you, partner. You have a choice. Blah Blah Blah.
"When I want to London in 1989, they told me I had to sign a release, so I did. I since have heard that many of my fellow inductees didn't."

In other words, after every paragraph break, you must reinforce the fact that we're in a quote by using opening quote marks for the new paragraph. However, long quotes of this nature aren't really the best approach in a written piece. Here's a better approach:

> ❖ *Improved choice:* "Don't let them do that to you, partner," Nelson advised. He explained that the new recruit actually had a choice and could refuse to sign a release.
> "When I want to London in 1989, they told me I had to sign a release, so I did," Nelson explained. "I since have heard that many of my fellow inductees didn't."

Don't simply quote at length, but take some of the information out of the quotes and use it as narration. This is a better approach in both fiction and nonfiction. Vary your delivery of the material.

Moreover, you might try to end a quote at the paragraph break or before and not let the quote run through to the next paragraph, simply because one out of every fifty readers—two percent—will miss the fact that the quote is continued. No, no reading experts have performed studies, but I feel the truth of this in my reading bones.

Questions in Quotes

Another very common mistake occurs in punctuating a question within a quote because somehow the writer can't distinguish between a question and a statement. For the question itself, we use a question mark, and for the statement, we use a period.

> ❖ *Wrong format:* "How do we go about this," he wondered out loud?
>
> ❖ *Correct format:* "How do we go about this?" he wondered out loud.

I'm not making this up. This is a very common mistake when the person writes a question within a statement.

Of course, another format dilemma sometimes comes up involving the question mark—where does the question mark go with quote marks?

Although we always place commas and periods inside quote marks even when this may seem absurd,* the question mark only goes inside the quote marks if the question is inside the quote. The mark goes outside the quotes if the question exceeds the boundaries of the quote marks.

> ❖ Correct: He asked, "Why should I go?"
>
> ❖ Correct: Did I hear him tell you, "I refuse to go"?
>
> ❖ Correct: Did he ask you, "Why should I go?"

In the last example above, notice that we only use one question mark at the end and not:

> ❖ *Incorrect:* Did he ask you, "Why should I go?"?

Note, too, that semicolons and colons go outside quotes:

> ❖ *Correct:* I replied, "Because I love you"; then I shot him.
>
> ❖ *Correct:* I replied, "Because I love you": Then I shot him.

By the way, the reason the comma and period go inside the quote marks is supposedly due to how type was originally set. The old way of setting "hot" type was for molten lead to run through a typography machine—the Linotype—with a typesetter typing in the words. The resulting pieces were placed together in a frame to form pages. The period and comma were the most fragile bits of type, and inserting them inside the end quote protected them better from being broken.

True or not, the story presents a picture of a time not as long gone as you might imagine. Typography lasted in some newsrooms until perhaps the late 1980s. I myself fondly recall working at a small newspaper in which the typographer (also known as a compositor) created hot type hour after hour making nearly no errors. Headlines were composed in a range of fonts from pieces of various larger-sized type kept in drawers.

Single Quote Marks

In the U.S., we use double quotes for quoting speech. Should any words need to be quoted within the quote, we use single quotation marks. This is the opposite of the convention in the United Kingdom (U.K.), so don't be surprised if you pick up a book in our common language that violates these rules.

> ❖ *Correct punctuation:* "I hope to read G. Miki's award-nominated story, 'War Crimes,' this weekend," Elaine told Herman.
>
> ❖ *Incorrect punctuation:* "I loved it when he said, "Hey, show some respect. We're talking about my father, not some character from Dickens." I love that episode," Jack told us.
>
> ❖ *Correct punctuation:* "I loved it when he said, 'Hey, show some respect. We're talking about my father, not some character from Dickens.' I love that episode," Jack told us.

Another sanctioned use of the single quotation mark is in headlines. Where we would ordinarily use a double quotation mark within the text, we instead use a single in a heading or headline, thus saving space—important perhaps in a large type size.

*Claim your free access to **www.firstwriter.com**: See p.263*

❖ *Correct punctuation:* Ford to City: 'Drop Dead'

Okay, that's not actually the correct punctuation because President Ford didn't literally say, "Drop dead" to New York City, and the actual headline read, "Ford to City: Drop Dead" without the single quote marks for a direct attribution. So, sue me. In theory, the punctuation is correct, although the headline is not true to life.

I looked all over for additional references to the use of pairs of single quotation marks and didn't find anything else, much to my surprise and dismay. I have personally used single quotes quite a lot to mark off key concepts. In doing so, I have apparently played fast and loose with punctuation. I have done wrong. Perhaps I have learned my lesson and will reform. Perhaps not. Something about the sets of single quote marks seems so subtle and ever so much more dignified than the double quotes. But don't listen to me. Don't make the horrible error I have made in trying to get away with things the others aren't allowed to do. Nary a one of us is above the Law. (And Lord spare us from the inappropriate capital.)

Key concepts *can* be placed in quotation marks to highlight them. These are sometimes also called "scare" or "apologetic" quotes. Do note that these are double quotes. Some people don't approve of the author's distancing himself from the quoted words, but we have many reasons to use the quotes to denote a special use of language.

❖ Correct use of scare quotes: They were amazed when John told them of the team's great "victory." (The team bombed, and John was being sarcastic.)

❖ Correct use of scare quotes: What does the instructor think of the use of the "scare quote"? (The offbeat term is marked off.)

Silent Speech

Sometimes we have a character in fiction thinking in exact speech, an approach I generally regard as inferior to quoting thoughts indirectly—try to reproduce your thoughts word for word and you'll

---

see why. At any rate, how do we quote this "silent speech"? Well, I'd suggest that we don't. We generally reserve quotes for speech delivered out loud, even whispered to oneself, while italic type is used for directly quoted internal thought. Webster's, however, says that silent speech may be placed in quotation marks (go figure) and that great blocks of italic should be avoided. By all means, avoid the rampant italic. I agree. The reader doesn't want to see too much of it. But to avoid long blocks of italic for silent speech, we can give only occasional, brief, direct quotes of thoughts.

Note, too, that we do use quotation marks for words we are quoting directly from print, rather than from spoken language. Similarly to silent speech, we also set off foreign phrases in italics. However, if the phrase has become common enough in English to simply be recognized, we don't use the italic. To finish up the concept of italics, since we're here, we also will very occasionally italicize a word for emphasis. We want to use extreme restraint in doing that, however, because we can't be there all the time ordering the reader around as to how to read each word. Perhaps our own emphasis, even if we're authoring the stories, is not the only one that could be made. Give the reader a tiny wedge of reading freedom. Moreover, in the vein of not repeating a noticeable pattern, avoiding an overuse of italic for emphasis is the better part of valor.

Italic has other uses, of course; any sequence in a book separated from the main concept or ongoing action can be set off in italics, from an interlude to a dream sequence. Italic is also used for book titles, magazine titles, and the titles of other long pieces of work.

By the way, these days we do italicize in our own manuscripts unless specifically requested to underline rather than italicize. We have the ability to easily produce italics with our computers, so why pretend we're at our typewriters?

Okay, and while I'm on the subject, these days we use one space in between sentences. Two spaces is what we inserted when we used typewriters. One space is sufficient since the computer does proportional and appropriate spacing.

The point here is really to simply get the very basic conventions correct,** which seems simple enough.

Other Style Issues With Quotes

When writing a lot of dialogue, in fiction in particular, we want to vary our format in citing the quotes. That is, we can indicate the speaker in more than one way.

❖ *Quote:* "Yes, actually," George said, moving to the bed and sitting down on the side closest to the door.

❖ *Quote*: "Yes, actually." George moved to the bed and sat down on the side closest to the door.

Which version is preferable depends on how the text reads, but if we have too many instances of "he said," and we don't really need another, then simply using the action to show the speaker is a nice option.

To be perfectly clear about what we mean by "words of citation," this phrase denotes that we use a word to indicate how, or simply that, words have been spoken.

❖ *Not a word of citation:* "I don't see how that would help," Robert frowned.

❖ *Not a word of citation:* "I don't see how that would help," Robert laughed.

We don't frown words and we don't laugh words. Nonetheless, sometimes that's how we want to write the sentence and cite the speech. We don't want to say: *"I don't see how that would help." Robert laughed.* We don't want to disconnect his laugh from the words he speaks. What should we do? We should disconnect the laugh or frown from the speech. That's what's appropriate. Sorry.

*Until today, I always said, "Commas and periods go inside the quote marks, always, always." Inevitably as one utters the word "always" or "never," one has the eerie feeling that an exception has crept in behind one's back. It's only on days like a Tuesday in spring when one finds out that that "except" is sitting on one's desk and grinning hideously. It has been in *The Chicago Manual of Style* all along.

When discussing philosophical concepts, says the official tome, single quote marks may be used to set off the idea. With such use, periods and commas go outside the single quote. Perhaps above, in this footnote, I should use singles quote with 'never' and 'always,' as I'm not entirely sure whether this is philosophical talk or not. But, of course 'never' and 'always' are pretty big concept words, so mayyybeee. (Okay, I just found out that linguists and mathematicians also use this convention, so that means, if we consider ourselves linguists here, the single quote with outside commas would be correct.)

Annoyingly as I begin to dig, I find that *CMOS* has another exception, an exception so picayune as to not be worth repeating— as if this one weren't picayune enough. Okay, I'll reveal it. The second exception has to do with quoting words already in print, such as: He said, "The quote from Shakespeare is, I believe, 'To be or not to be'." In this case the period goes outside the quote mark because the actual quote from Shakespeare doesn't end there and the writer doesn't want to confuse the reader into thinking it does. There— now are you happy?

** Here, the "get the convention correct" seems to be wrong in that we might expect to "get the convention correctly." However, no, this is an elliptical use, with words left out. We really mean "Let's 'get' the convention so that our usage is correct."

Exercise

Part I.
Correct any of the following that are wrong:
1. He liked being able to say to their friends, *Why don't you come with us to Florida this weekend? Barbara and I are flying down in our private jet. I'm the pilot.*
2. "He isn't here," she told the man, "I'm his associate. Maybe I can help you."
3. "Mr. Ryder is an investigator"? the voice at the other end asked hesitantly.

4. "Win a Ruger Mini-14," the cover coaxed seductively.
5. Did Eric, like the publisher of the magazine, believe that "Tailhook" had been a witch-hunt, "all smoke, no fire?"
6. He smiled at her, so she went on. "I served in the Air Force for ten years and I'm a licensed flight instructor—multi-engine."
7. He was so somber that she wanted to say something silly, such as "mum's" the word but instead she nodded with a solemnity exactly equal to his own.
8. "I'm sorry for the guy." Said Smeis, "I'm sorry for the widow, especially. But Rotz wasn't popular out here at Sandhurst, I have to tell you."
9. "Yes," Smeis nodded, "but over North Vietnam."
10. He might ask a few awkward questions such as where did you get this airplane.
11. We traditionally use the expression 20/20 to mean that some-one has absolutely perfect vision, either metaphorically or in actuality.
12. Told the outline was "stamped 'best seller,' " and asked for pages, Bradford admitted she hadn't even started the book.
13. Now that Dove and his unit had the file, "The case wasn't one we were going to give up on."
14. I woke up at 2 a.m. Tuesday morning trying to remember what I had just dreamed. What was it? I was having a leisurely dinner with friends, and then, suddenly, I realized I had a boat to catch. I hurried over to the waterfront. I was just about in time, I thought, but a moment later, I found out the shocking truth—the boat had departed.

Part II.

Put the quotes and any other needed capitals, lower case, or punctuation in this portion of my novel New Pacific. *Second part of the exercise—if the novel looks good, buy a copy. (Joking, joking—it's out of print.)*

Ah, thankfully Murmured the subordinate. Although the plane manufacture was our own. I hope responsibility doesn't devolve upon the company. Najita grinned happily at his subaltern. Your schooling with us has not gone to any waste, Tanizaki-san. I'm glad to have called the right man to Singapore. A wan smile crossed Takashi's classically handsome features. The name Tanizaki was usually reserved for his own father, someone who had once advised his middle son, keep a low profile. Anything higher and you'll have to duck. Where is Dr. Sato, anyway asked Takashi, looking around the office and taking the visitor's chair, while Najita seated himself at the master computing station. Oh yes, indeed. That's part of the question. Najita sounded a note of mock bemusement. Takashi pointed his head in the direction of the security chief. Brought up in a former enclave of the Japanese empire, not all his habits were quite Japanese, but he had learned not to look at a superior directly. He focused on the console beside his boss. What were those...things...in there he inquired quietly? Yes, yes, that, too. Najita booted up the puter and began to idly thumb through the stored files—one of those security habits that Takashi, also, practiced when the occasion arose. We don't know where Dr. Sato is right this minute Najita continued. One of the things I'd like you to do would be to find him. And going back to the issue of implants that we raised before, think how easy it would be to uncover our subject today, if he had an implant inside his tissues. Yes, an embedded can be surgically removed, but it would have given us an edge in locating him when he first disappeared. Which was? Five days ago—or maybe before. Oh, yes, probably. During the holidays, he wasn't expected to show up at work—although during previous days off, he liked to check in, watch over his "experiments". But not this time. Najita paused, lost in his own personal reverie, his big hands still mechanically roving over the keyboard in front of him. Defection asked Takashi? Or a kidnapping. Hmmm... oh, it doesn't matter at this point. If you find him, we can bring him back, either way. Dialogue without quote marks is weird, isn't it? Though I must say the book looks awfully interesting...

Answers

Part I.

1. He liked being able to say to their friends, *Why don't you come with us to Florida this weekend? Barbara and I are*

flying down in our private jet. I'm the pilot.
He liked being able to say to their friends, "Why don't you
come with us to Florida this weekend? Barbara and I are
flying down in our private jet. I'm the pilot." (No italic.)

2.   "He isn't here," she told the man, "I'm his associate. Maybe
I can help you."
"He isn't here," she told the man. "I'm his associate.
Maybe I can help you."

3.   "Mr. Ryder is an investigator"? the voice at the other end
asked hesitantly.
"Mr. Ryder is an investigator?" the voice at the other end
asked hesitantly.

4.   "Win a Ruger Mini-14," the cover coaxed seductively.
Correct.

5.   Did Eric, like the publisher of the magazine, believe that
"Tailhook" had been a witch-hunt, "all smoke, no fire?"
Did Eric, like the publisher of the magazine, believe that
Tailhook had been a "witch-hunt," "all smoke, no fire"?

6.   He smiled at her, so she went on. "I served in the Air Force
for ten years and I'm a licensed flight instructor—multi-
engine."
He smiled at her, so she went on, "I served in the Air Force
for ten years, and I'm a licensed flight instructor—multi-
engine.(Actually the first version is also correct. This really
depends on the author's intent.)

7.   He was so somber that she wanted to say something silly,
such as "mum's" the word but instead she nodded with a
solemnity exactly equal to his own.
He was so somber that she wanted to say something silly,
such as "mum's the word," but instead she nodded with a
solemnity exactly equal to his own. (While the clause "mum's
the word" might be written here in italic instead of quotes,
since it's NOT spoken, I chose quotes because she MIGHT
HAVE spoken it.—We do have some room for variation.)

8.   "I'm sorry for the guy." Said Smeis, "I'm sorry for the
widow, especially. But Rotz wasn't popular out here at
Sandhurst, I have to tell you."
"I'm sorry for the guy," said Smeis. "I'm sorry for the
widow, especially. But Rotz wasn't popular out here at

Sandhurst, I have to tell you."
9. "Yes," Smeis nodded, "but over North Vietnam."
"Yes." Smeis nodded. "But over North Vietnam."
10. He might ask a few awkward questions such as where did you get this airplane.
He might ask a few awkward questions such as, "Where did you get this airplane?"
11. We traditionally use the expression 20/20 to mean that someone has absolutely perfect vision, either metaphorically or in actuality.
We traditionally use the expression "20/20" to mean that someone has absolutely perfect vision, either metaphorically or in actuality.
12. Told the outline was "stamped 'best seller,'" and asked for pages, Bradford admitted she hadn't even started the book.
Correct.
13. Now that Dove and his unit had the file, "The case wasn't one we were going to give up on."
Now that Dove and his unit had the file: "The case wasn't one we were going to give up on." (The colon is a fair enough, though not commonplace, choice.)
14. I woke up at 2 a.m. Tuesday morning trying to remember what I had just dreamed. What was it? I was having a leisurely dinner with friends, and then, suddenly, I realized I had a boat to catch. I hurried over to the waterfront. I was just about in time, I seemed to think, but a moment later, I found out the shocking truth—the boat had departed.
I woke up at 2 a.m. Tuesday morning trying to remember what I had just dreamed. What was it? I was having a leisurely dinner with friends, and then, suddenly, I realized I had a boat to catch. I hurried over to the waterfront. I was just about in time, I thought, but a moment later, I found out the shocking truth—the boat had departed. *(In other words, the dream is in italic and that sets off the dream so we don't think the events were from the real world.)*

Part II.

"Ah, thankfully," murmured the subordinate. "Although the plane manufacture was our own. I hope responsibility doesn't devolve upon the company."

Najita grinned happily at his subaltern. "Your schooling with us has not gone to any waste, Tanizaki-san. I'm glad to have called the right man to Singapore."

A wan smile crossed Takashi's classically handsome features. The name "Tanizaki" was usually reserved for his own father, someone who had once advised his middle son, "Keep a low profile. Anything higher and you'll have to duck."

"Where is Dr. Sato, anyway?" asked Takashi, looking around the office and taking the visitor's chair, while Najita seated himself at the master computing station.

"Oh yes, indeed. That's part of the question." Najita sounded a note of mock bemusement.

Takashi pointed his head in the direction of the security chief. Brought up in a former enclave of the Japanese empire, not all his habits were quite Japanese, but he had learned not to look at a superior directly. He focused on the console beside his boss.

"What were those...things...in there?" he inquired quietly.

"Yes, yes, that, too." Najita booted up the puter and began to idly thumb through the stored files—one of those security habits that Takashi, also, practiced when the occasion arose.

"We don't know where Dr. Sato is right this minute," Najita continued. "One of the things I'd like you to do would be to find him. And going back to the issue of implants that we raised before, think how easy it would be to uncover our subject today, if he had an implant inside his tissues. Yes, an embedded can be surgically removed, but it would have given us an edge in locating him when he first disappeared."

"Which was?"

"Five days ago—or maybe before. Oh, yes, probably. During the holidays, he wasn't expected to show up at work—although during previous days off, he liked to check in, watch over his 'experiments.' But not this time." Najita paused, lost in his own personal reverie, his big hands still mechanically roving over the keyboard in front of him.

"Defection?" asked Takashi. "Or a kidnapping?"

"Hmmm... oh, it doesn't matter at this point. If you find him, we can bring him back, either way."

Punctuation Unmasked

Asking an editor what error he likes least is like asking a bartender what drink he least likes to see spilled on the bar—the spills all need mopping up. But one thing that frequently sets my teeth on edge is the unnecessary comma. For instance: "Bob took a sip, and set the drink down." The comma is supposed to indicate that the actions in the two parts of the sentence are not simultaneous, I suppose, but doesn't the word "and" also serve that function? If you cut either the comma or the word "and," don't you get the same result?

—Gordon Van Gelder

Editor/Publisher, The Magazine of Fantasy & Science Fiction

Probably the greatest numbers of mistakes in writing are made with punctuation. Yet we use barely more than a handful of punctuation marks regularly, and the rules regarding these marks are really quite limited. Of course, I don't think we should worry *overly* about all the niceties of punctuation, as most people don't seem to be able to punctuate correctly, and certainly few agents, editors, or readers know all the rules.

Don't think I'm being dismissive of punctuation, though. The above is the reality. The other reality is that punctuation is a deep, complex study, well worth pursuing for those who have the intestinal fortitude. The more appropriate your punctuation, the more "unseen" it becomes. Correct punctuation doesn't distract the reader, but aids him in understanding our meaning without a lot of fanfare. If we want to write really well, we should learn how to punctuate seamlessly.

I'd like to discuss the basics of punctuation in brief in this section. The question of quotation marks isn't covered here, however, because the consideration is a large one. I talk about quotes in the previous chapter.

Commas

The most frequently used punctuation mark is the comma. Learn to use the comma well, and your work will sparkle with the sheen of well-rubbed polish. Use the comma poorly, and the hapless reader will be stuttering all over the place, pausing like a driver at a misplaced traffic sign.

The comma has numerous distinct functions, as well as applications that are either discouraged or outright groaned at by the knowing (watch very carefully for those).

With Coordinating Conjunctions

The comma can be teamed with a coordinating conjunction (*and*, *but*, *or*, *so*, *yet*, *nor*, *for*) to join two independent clauses. The key here is the phrase "independent clauses." Just because we have a coordinating conjunction doesn't mean we need a comma. If you're not bridging two clauses that can otherwise each stand on its own, decide if a comma is warranted in order to provide greater clarity or a needed pause.

> ❖ *Correct:* Buried in the rubble, Amy Zelson Mundorff thought her time had come, but the next day, with two black eyes, she was back on the job.
>
> ❖ *Correct:* Forensic anthropology is a subset of physical anthropology and is a field that doesn't offer many jobs.

In sentence one we joint two independent clauses with a comma and a coordinating conjunction: "Amy Zelson Mundorff thought her time had come, **but** the next day, with two black eyes, she was back on the job." In the second sentence, the "and" doesn't need a comma because we aren't joining two independent clauses: "...**and** is a field that doesn't offer many jobs."

Warning: Don't use a comma to join two independent clauses without a coordinating conjunction. This is wrong and is called a comma splice, which sounds okay, but definitely isn't. A comma splice produces the deplorable run-on sentence. (Head for the hills, boys.)

❖ *Wrong:* Skeletons have characteristics that individualize them, pins and plates inserted during surgeries come with serial numbers that can be tracked.

❖ *Correct:* Skeletons have characteristics that individualize them. For instance, pins and plates inserted during surgeries come with serial numbers that can be tracked.

❖ *Correct:* Skeletons have characteristics that individualize them; for instance, pins and plates inserted during surgeries come with serial numbers that can be tracked.

And, yes, we can start a sentence with a coordinating conjunction.

We may also place a comma after the initial coordinating conjunction, but usually we don't. If we use the comma after an initial coordinating conjunction, we shouldn't do so habitually. That comma use is a quirk that can be annoying if repeated too often.

❖ *Correct:* And, not all the bones Mundorff receives are even human.

❖ *Correct:* And not all the bones Mundorff receives are even human.

❖ *Correct, but annoying:* And, not all the bones Mundorff receives are even human, since many are

---

> animal bones. But, some of the bones thought to be animal bones are actually the bones of infants. Yet, some officers are reluctant to bring them in.

Direct Address

We use the comma in all instances of direct address. This is a rule that seems to cause many writers to falter, though the use is obviously both simple and clear. When one person speaks to another, calling the other by some sort of name, formal or informal, we use a comma for direct address.

> ❖ *Correct:* "John, will you get me an ashtray?"
>
> ❖ *Correct:* "So you said, sweetheart, repeatedly."
>
> ❖ *Correct:* "Please, officer, may I go now?"

Interrupting Modifying Phrases

We use commas to set off interrupting adjective phrases. An interrupting adjective phrase would be a phrase out of its expected position in the sentence.

> ❖ *Correct, expected position:* Her old, worn dress had been washed and ironed.
>
> ❖ *Correct, interrupting position:* Her dress, old and worn, had been washed and ironed.

The adverb phrase, when interrupting, may or may not also take a comma pair, such as in this very sentence.

> ❖ *Correct, expected position:* He went to the dentist without a fuss.

> ❖ *Correct, interrupting position:* He went without a fuss to the dentist.
>
> ❖ *Correct, interrupting position:* The adverb phrase, when interrupting, may or may not take a comma pair.

Introductory Phrases

Introductory *phrases*—as opposed to *clauses*—may or may not take a comma, depending on length and on personal style. With four or five words or more in an introductory phrase, we usually use a comma.

> ❖ *Correct:* After class let's have a drink.
>
> ❖ *Correct:* After class, let's have a drink.
>
> ❖ *Correct:* After the end of today's sociology class, let's have a drink.

Personally, I use a comma after a two-word phrase such as "after class." I feel that a switch occurs that will be well served by a comma when moving from the prepositional (adverb) phrase to the main clause. I'm sure, though, that, on occasion, I would prefer the other format, depending on the words and how they "read."

Participle Phrases

We use a comma after an introductory (inverted) participle phrase, but not necessarily when the phrase is in its expected, later position in the sentence. Then, the comma is optional.

> ❖ *Incorrect:* Having signed the papers Phoebe went for a run.

❖ *Correct:* Having signed the papers, Phoebe went for a run.

❖ *Correct:* Phoebe went for a run taking the papers to be mailed.

❖ *Correct:* Phoebe went for a run, taking the papers to be mailed.

Often, I prefer the comma before the participle phrase that comes in its proper position in the sentence. But sometimes the comma really doesn't seem necessary. We want to be able to form our own judgment about these optional commas, although we might change our minds on the next draft of the piece. I have also found that my entire attitude toward commas will change from time to time. Sometimes I feel the use of all optional commas adds polish, while other times I think the extra commas look too "fussy." Let your commas suit your own taste, unless they are required by a rule. Then know the rule.

Single Introductory Word

We also most often use a comma after a single introductory word. But sometimes we will not want that much of a pause.

❖ *Correct:* Frequently, the president and Mrs. Bush travel on Air Force One.

❖ *Correct:* However, President Bush will probably not be successful in changing Social Security in the way that he would like.

❖ *Correct:* Definitely he won't.

❖ *Correct:* Definitely, he won't.

Introductory or Interrupting Adverb Clauses

We use commas to set off inverted introductory or interrupting adverb clauses.

> ❖ *Correct introductory adverb clause:* When Lt. Parker responded to the call, he found the mother and daughter tied up in the closet.

Note that this introductory wording constitutes a dependent clause, also known as a subordinate clause. The dependent/subordinate clause can't stand on its own, though it has a subject ("Lt. Parker") and verb ("responded").

> ❖ *Correct interrupting adverb clause:* I can, if you want, deliver this personally.

City and State

We use a comma to separate city and state.

> ❖ *Correct:* Dr. Johnson has a practice in Miami, Florida.

We also often use abbreviations for states—as set forth in a publication's individual style guide or using the postal two-letter abbreviations. We will generally, too, just say "Miami" and not add the state, because everyone knows that we mean Florida.

Items in a List

We use commas to separate items in a list.* I'm sure by now (the 21st century) everyone has fixed in mind the idea that the last comma before the coordinating conjunction can be dropped. This is not wholly accurate, and, happily, the trend is back toward the use of that comma.

The Chicago Manual of Style notes that we use commas to separate every item, from first to last (bravo). Strunk and White (which is the elliptical reference to a book entitled *The Elements of Style*, written by William Strunk Jr. and revised by E. B. White) agrees (yes, "agrees," because we're referring to the book and not the authors) that we should use commas before the coordinating conjunction finishing the list.

> ❖   *Correct:* I had eggs, cheese, toast, and coffee.

Naturally, nothing is ever really that simple, and Strunk and White adds that for a company name, the writer should follow the firm's preference, such as Blake, Cassels & Graydon LLP, or even McDermott Will & Emery LLP. Of course we should.

But "the serial comma," as the last comma before the conjunction has come to be called (also "the Oxford comma" as well as "the Harvard comma") has its detractors. Pick up the Associated Press style book, whatever the title of its current version is, and you'll find a rather confounding rule.

> ❖   *Correct to AP style:* I had eggs, cheese, toast and coffee. Yet the AP style book adds that the serial comma should be picked up again if (a) the phrases are complex or (b) an element in the series itself requires a conjunction (oh brother).
>
> ❖   *Correct to AP style:* I visited the Tower of London with John, Buckingham Palace with Mr. and Mrs. Reynolds, and the Houses of Parliament with Becky.
>
> ❖   *Correct to AP style:* I had juice, toast, eggs and bacon, and coffee.

This means that the writer would sometimes use the serial comma and sometimes not, even in the same paragraph?

> ❖ *Correct to AP style:* I looked at the company's books, its annual report, and its staffing records and personnel files. The company has the science, the finances and the promotional capacity to do the job. However, it's missing the updated technology to do the more complex calculations, the trained support workers to fulfill the contract, and the other necessary lower-level workers to produce the final product.

Personally, I find this mix and match of serial comma and not serial comma a little bit off-putting. One thing we try for as writers is consistency in style. We don't sometimes use an ampersand and sometimes spell out the word "and." We try to do the same thing all the time so that our use of these elements slides in under the radar.

Of course, mere consistency is probably not the best reason to employ the serial comma. Instead, the most compelling argument might be that the serial comma works. (All grammarphiles dance in celebration at such a pronouncement.) A final comma before the conjunction does a very nice job of separating items in a list with the least confusion for the reader. I'm not sure why we ever decided to drop that comma, but I know the trend arose in my lifetime and that the elimination of that mark saves nothing, but certainly adds more than its share of distraction for the wordhound.

Short, Independent Clauses in a Series

We use commas to separate short, independent clauses in a series. This rule is kind of an exception to the rule, because most independent clauses are simply separated by semicolons. But when the independent clauses are short and several, they are treated just as phrases in a series would be.

> ❖ *Correct:* We went, we ate lunch, we came home.

With Multiple Adjectives

We sometimes use commas with two or more adjectives before a noun to make the reading easier, but this depends on whether the adjectives are "independent" from one another, that is, whether they modify the noun independently.

> ❖   *Correct:* The old, rusted stove attracted my attention.

Since we can say, "the old stove" as well as "the rusted stove," that indicates we can probably use a comma between the adjectives. Another sign we might go by is whether we can use an "and" between the adjectives—"the old and rusted stove." Be aware, though, that neither of these rules of thumb is surefire.

> ❖   *Correct:* The red brick house stood out from the other homes along the street.

We don't use the comma, although we could say "the red house," and "the brick house." We can't say "the red and brick house," however, because that doesn't sound right, and because we really don't want to cut "brick" off from the adjective "red." These two adjectives are actually quite connected as the brick itself is red (which is what makes the house red). On the other hand, we don't want to hyphenate and say "the red-brick house" because we don't want to just describe the brick as red; we want to describe the house as red as well. Our best choice here then is to neither separate the words with a comma nor stick them together with the hyphen.

In terms of the other rule of thumb, using the "and" test:

> ❖   *Correct:* She wore a pretty, pink dress.

Here, we can say "a pretty dress" and "a pink dress" but we can't say "a pretty and pink dress" because that sounds awkward. However, while we could say "pretty pink" without a comma, what does that imply about the meaning? Are we saying that the dress is pretty or that the pink is pretty? If we're saying the dress is pretty, then the comma would be appropriate. If we're saying the pink is pretty, we don't want the comma.

Certainly our pondering the comma presupposes that anyone actually cares about the comma when reading the sentence. Of course, often people do care and making the meaning clear is a very good thing. However, here, don't be surprised if the reader will simply see the word "pretty" and the word "pink," and he will visualize the dress as both pretty and pink, making the comma question moot.

In essence, then, using the comma with the adjectives is a decision we make by virtue of our familiarity with the language and by knowing how the punctuation sounds (see the chapter on reading punctuation).

Comma Don'ts

Commas, because they interrupt the flow, should also be avoided at times. For instance, using a comma after a linking verb is wrong.

❖ *Wrong:* The only thing I don't like about Ted is, his insistence on going to the movies on Fridays.

❖ *Correct:* The only thing I don't like about Ted is his insistence on going to the movies on Fridays.

Since the "is" serves a *linking* function, we don't want the pause—the separation—created by the comma.

Don't use a comma between the verb and its object.

❖ *Wrong:* I saw him hit, her.

❖ *Correct:* I saw him hit her.

While that comma position might seem farfetched to many of us, I find this type of use in students' writing, so don't discount the possibility that someone will place a comma that inappropriately.

Don't use a comma between a subject and a verb, unless you have an interrupting clause and a comma *pair*.

> ❖ *Wrong:* Either George or the one who came after him in line, was the last to receive bread.
>
> ❖ *Correct:* Either George or the one who came after him in line was the last to receive bread.
>
> ❖ *Correct:* George, who is my roommate, was the last to receive bread.

Don't use a comma before a parenthesis (I see this one sometimes, too). And don't use a comma just prior to the end parenthesis.

> ❖ *Incorrect*: Well-written, (although the author won an award for a prior book), the novel and its characters won me over.
>
> ❖ *Incorrect:* Well-written (although a prior book received the Pulitzer rather than this one,) the novel and its characters won me over.
>
> ❖ *Correct:* Well-written (although a prior book received the Pulitzer rather than this one), the novel and its characters won me over.

Restrictive Versus Nonrestrictive

At this time we have to discuss restrictive and nonrestrictive words, phrases, and clauses, which are generally confusing to most of us. I don't think they would be so confusing if we didn't call them "restrictive" and "nonrestrictive," since the naming throws off most people, rather than the concept.

Let me define the two words and then explain the idea. The only really important part is to get the punctuation right by adhering to the concept.

A restrictive word, phrase, or clause identifies the person or thing being talked about, making the identification material mandatory— we need that identification, which *restricts* whatever is being discussed. We don't use a comma because we don't want to separate the restricting identifier from that which is being identified. The nonrestrictive elements, on the other hand, "merely" give additional information about something that has already been identified. We do use commas with these nonessential elements.

> ❖ *Correct:* I gave him the desk that I wasn't using.
>
> ❖ *Correct:* I gave him the desk, which I wasn't using.

The "which" versus "that" distinction is a major one that (or comma which) I discuss frequently with students (end comma if we used a comma before a which) because we often didn't learn this early on in school. In this example, the only distinction we can really see is that a "which" takes a comma. But the distinction also involves the pause for the comma, so the two sentences read differently. Strictly speaking, we can say that in the first sentence the "I" person has more than one desk and needs to define the desk given more closely—"the desk that I wasn't using." In the second sentence, we deduce that we're only discussing one, single desk. We don't know if the "I" person has another or not, but that's not relevant. The "I" person has generously given away a particular desk, the one under discussion.

Let me just say this without using the words restrictive and nonrestrictive: If you have a which, you almost certainly will precede that with a comma.

However, in order to distress you even further, I have to add that sometimes we can have a which without a comma, when the which is used as an alternative to another "that."

> ❖ *Correct:* I hope in that case you will take the desk which I set aside for you. The others are sold.

Of course you can also reframe the sentence and retain only one "that," instead of using the "which." However, sometimes that doesn't work as well as using the "which."

Have you gone nuts yet? Well, to make matters worse, we'll discuss restrictive and nonrestrictive appositives. Remember, though, the most important thing is to get the punctuation right, not keep in mind the meaning of the words "restrictive" and "nonrestrictive"—or even "appositive"—phooey on the names.

The correct punctuation can often simply come from your understanding of how the sentence reads.

Appositives are a further definition of a noun or pronoun. Appositives can be either restrictive or nonrestrictive. (Oy.)

> ❖ *Restrictive:* My brother Jack is a musician.
>
> ❖ *Nonrestrictive:* My brother, Jack, is a musician.

In the first case above, the speaker has more than one brother, but is discussing only the brother named Jack. In the second sentence, the speaker has one brother, Jack.

> ❖ *Restrictive:* John in the corner came with Suzi.
>
> ❖ *Nonrestrictive:* John, the boy in the corner, came with Suzi.
>
> ❖ *Nonrestrictive:* The boy in the corner, John, came with Suzi.
>
> ❖ *Restrictive:* John is one of the boys who came with Suzi.

> ❖ *Nonrestrictive clause:* John, who came with Suzi, is her cousin.

Actually, this leads us to the last comma "don't." Don't use a comma before a restrictive participle.

> ❖ *Incorrect:* Lena shielded her eyes and squinted at a man, wearing jogging shorts and a faded NYPD t-shirt.
>
> ❖ *Correct:* Lena shielded her eyes and squinted at a man wearing jogging shorts and a faded NYPD t-shirt.

He's wearing the shorts, not Lena, and that's a restrictive phrase.

For Clarity

We use a comma when one will make our meaning clearer. That could be any type of insertion, and while that's the author's call, we want to be fairly positive we're adding to the sentence clarity. Here are a couple of examples:

> ❖ *Muddled:* At this time of day only two months before I would've been happily listening to some country music, checking emails, and preparing for bed.
>
> ❖ *Clearer:* At this time of day only two months before, I would've been happily listening to some country music, checking emails, and preparing for bed.

I call the first sentence "muddled" because, when I read it for the first time, I read the words "before I" together, only to have to go back and reread. Now maybe *I'm* muddled and the sentence was fine, but if I'm muddled, other readers will be, too. We can catch and fix some of these types of things when we go through a further draft of our work. Of course, sometimes we catch the little glitches after the piece is already handed in or in print, which is why many authors don't read their writing after it's published.

❖ *Muddled:* Her Narcotics Anonymous support group meetings were helping her along with her sister Clare and Clare's husband, John.

❖ *Clearer:* Her Narcotics Anonymous support group meetings were helping her, along with her sister Clare and Clare's husband, John.

Yes, all right. I'm the muddled one, but in reading the first sentence, I thought the meetings were helping her along. They were not. They, along with her sister, were helping her. Thus, I put in the comma.

❖ *Tricky:* The wind blew dirt, leaves, and nameless detritus inside onto the lawn.

❖ *Clearer:* The wind blew dirt, leaves, and nameless detritus inside, onto the lawn.

❖ *Tricky:* Are these people you know and have contact numbers for for a secondary comment?

❖ *Clearer:* Are these people you know and have contact numbers for, for a secondary comment?

For the want of a comma a kingdom was lost. (Okay, attributed to Ben Franklin, the observation is that for the want of a nail a kingdom was lost, but that's so yesterday.)

For a Deliberate Pause

Clarity is one thing and desired emphasis with a pause is another. The author isn't always entitled to that pause, as some spots don't

---

permit a comma (see the anti-comma rules above). However, when a comma might be optional, we can insert one simply for that little reader breath and the "punch" a pause for breath may give the sentence.

> ❖ *Correct:* She thought, well, so what. Let him. What the heck.

Can you believe all the above describes comma use? That's way too much to integrate into one's worldview in any short period of time. Seriously. No one expects you to now know everything about using commas. Keep looking up the rules when you find yourself confused. You can place a bookmark at the first page of the punctuation section, if you like. (My best friend would say, "I can? I know I can. If I want to.")

Periods

The period goes lots of places, obviously, including at the end of most sentences, but also after abbreviations and titles: U.S., Huntsville (Ala.), Pfc. Nadera, John F. Kennedy, U.N. (only as an adjective, not as a noun), Mr. and Mrs. Kaminsky, R. Dagnese, Robert Wayts Jr., Ph.D., L.A., etc.

Periods are omitted many places as well: UNESCO (United Nations Educational, Scientific and Cultural Organization), UFO (unidentified flying object), LSD (lysergic acid diethylamide), EST (Eastern Standard Time), NFL (National Football League), JFK (John F. Kennedy).

If acronyms, such as the above, are commonly used and well known, the period(s) is (are) dropped. That choice, however, isn't the individual writer's—odd, but true. Who makes these fateful decisions? The people who write dictionaries. And, to think, they aren't certified, elected, or appointed by a governmental body, and have no commonly acknowledged requirements for their positions. Mind boggling, isn't it?

Other places where we use the common but fairly uncomplicated period are after a number or letter in some types of lists and in outlines (a form of list).

Symptoms of the disorder include:

1. persistent hyperactivity,
2. impulsivity, and
3. inattention.

I. Question one
A. Supporting hypothesis one
1. First detail
2. Second detail
B. Second supporting hypothesis

A variant of the period is the ever-popular ellipsis. The basic ellipsis consists of three dots, but we will find different advice on how to enter that into a sentence. Some say we type the ellipsis as space, period, space, period, space, period, space. Some say we simply keyboard in the three dots in a row. And others suggest that we use a shortcut provided by our word processor: Alt-Ctrlperiod in Microsoft Word.

We use an ellipsis to indicate that words have been omitted from quotes, or that a speaker's voice has trailed off (as opposed to the speaker's being interrupted, which requires a dash), or to indicate that one's thoughts have trailed off. If the sentence ends before the speaker trails off, we first include a period for the end of the sentence, inserting the ellipsis afterward. For an omission within a quotation, say of several sentences, we place the ellipsis between the included pieces of text with a space on either side. If we omit part of a quoted sentence and then begin again in the middle of a sentence, the text after the ellipsis starts with a lower case.

Question Marks

The question mark naturally goes after a question, generally wherever one is found, including in the middle of a sentence.

> ❖ *Correct:* Was this a giant in front of him? the boy wondered. (People have a lot of trouble with this one, so mark this down in your mental notebook and don't forget.)

A rhetorical question receives a question mark or an exclamation point.

> ❖ *Correct:* Will you get off your high horse and answer my question?
>
> ❖ *Correct:* Will you get off your high horse and answer my question!

Exclamation Points

The exclamation point is used for emphasis, often with interjections, and can be used within a sentence as well as to end one.

> ❖ *Correct:* Boy! what a great movie that was.
>
> ❖ *Correct:* Boy, what a great movie that was!
>
> ❖ *Correct:* Boy, what a great movie that was.

The real problem with the exclamation point is its overuse. The exclamation point tends to add a "gosh, golly, gee" tone to the writing, which will inevitably irritate the editor, if not the reader. The words themselves should be used to transmit the emotion at least the great majority of the time. Consider the old saw in regard to exercise: "When I feel the urge, I just wait for it to go away." We might try that approach when faced with an impulse to insert the exclamation point. Resist, resist.

Semicolons

The semicolon is more common than it ought to be. That is, the semicolon should be as rare as hen's teeth, or just about—but writers today are in love with the formerly arcane mark. That's because being able to tell when the semicolon should be used between independent clauses is not as simple as it seems. Often, the semicolon *may* be used, but isn't really needed. If it's not needed, don't use it. Once we see when a semicolon *should* be used, we will experience an *aha* moment of illumination. The insight produced will be similar to that which arose when we "got" something such as sushi or turn-of-the (19th)-century architecture.

Please remember, the semicolon isn't simply a mark we may employ at will. Very specific rules govern semicolon use. We can't just toss one into a sentence when we feel the sentence needs a strong interruption (gak). Here are the rules.

The semicolon may be used to join/separate two independent clauses that are very closely related.

> ❖ *Correct:* He wanted to go; she wanted to stay.
>
> ❖ *Correct:* He wanted to go. She wanted to stay.
>
> ❖ *Correct:* He wanted to go, but she wanted to stay.
>
> ❖ *Correct:* He wanted to go; but she wanted to stay.
>
> ❖ *Incorrect:* He wanted to go; because she wanted to stay.
>
> ❖ *Correct:* He wanted to go because she wanted to stay.

The semicolon may be used *with* a coordinating conjunction or *instead* of one. The semicolon can't be used with a subordinating conjunction, however, because then we no longer have the required two (or more) independent clauses. Similarly, the semicolon may also be used with conjunctive adverbs or transitional phrases.

> ❖ *Correct:* He wanted to go; however, she wanted to stay.
>
> ❖ *Correct:* He wanted to go; all in all, she wanted to stay.

The only use for a semicolon between dependent phrases or clauses is when separating a list of complex (with internal punctuation), complicated, or lengthy elements.

> ❖ *Correct:* Please set out a half can of the food in the cupboard twice a day, plus a half cup of the dry food in the morning; fresh water at least twice a day; and the rawhide bone while you are in the house.

Colons

We use a colon after an independent clause (or occasionally even after a phrase) to announce that something connected with the first bit follows. If what follows is a full sentence, we can capitalize the sentence, and that is a preferred style, especially if what follows is more than one single sentence. If what follows is not a full sentence or is a list, we don't capitalize.

We try to use the colon judiciously, because it, like the semicolon, is a piece of punctuation that draws attention to itself and becomes a distraction if overused.

A colon is also used in one form of writing the time (12:15) and in some types of formal and footnoted citations of reference sources, as well as to introduce long quotations of material (often indented). The colon is used after the salutation in any formal letter, such as a business letter.

> ❖ *Correct:* I want to clean the house: sweep the floors, dust, and wipe down the sinks.
>
> ❖ *Incorrect:* I want to: sweep, dust, and clean the sinks.
>
> ❖ *Correct:* I want to sweep, dust, and clean the sinks.

The second example above is not correct because the colon here actually interrupts the sentence. (The effect is one of placing random punctuation in the middle of a sentence.)

❖ *Correct:* I have a great idea: We'll go to New York for the holidays.

❖ *Correct:* I have a great idea: we'll to New York for the holidays.

❖ *Incorrect:* I have a great idea: we'll go to New York for the holidays. We'll see some shows.

❖ *Correct:* I have a great idea: We'll go to New York for the holidays. We'll see some shows.

❖ *Correct:* Because of one tiny detail: Rudy said no.

This last example shows that we can use a phrase with a colon, even though we generally first have an independent clause.

Dashes

Every writer loves the dash, and some of us love it a little too much. The dash is a handy way of saying to the world: I give up on punctuation, so sue me. The dash isn't really ever mandated, but it's often called for. The dash can set off parenthetical remarks of a certain kind. The use of the dash relates more to how punctuation reads, discussed elsewhere, than to any set of punctuation rules.

The dash is often called an "em dash," derived from the time when hot lead was poured into type. The "em" is a hot type unit of measurement. The dash or "em dash"—as opposed to the "en" dash—is made on the computer by keying in two hyphens side by side or inserting the symbol. We don't leave a space on either side of the em dash, which butts up against the words beside it. Most frequently the em dash comes in pairs.

An em dash also shows an interruption, such as when speech is interrupted by another speaker or an event. " 'I wanted to—' Rod began to say. But just then the boys heard the sound of a car backfiring."

Here are some examples of em dash use:

❖ *Correct:* I was so irked by Sid—and everything—that when I got outside, I lit a cigarette.

❖ *Correct:* Nearly every week, I hear of a new junior gold exploration company—and I write a column for *The Gold Dust Standard,* so I should already know them all.

❖ *Correct:* Being reasonable doesn't mean simply being able to offer "reasons" for events, but means being able to predict and reproduce (on paper) the operation of the world as we know it—according to both its physical and social laws.

The em dash in the first example is being used to present an "aside," which can be described as a bit of commentary added to the main idea. In the second example, the em dash is used to add emphasis to the conclusion of the sentence. The dash is more "explosive" that a comma would be here. In the third example, the em dash is used as a colon might be—to present further material for consideration.

If we use Microsoft Word to create a document, often the em dash will be inserted for two hyphens as we type (after we check the option that we want this done)—and then if we go back and make a correction, we might be stuck with the double hyphen when we finish our writing. Does that matter? Mostly that would depend on how fastidious we want to be. We can do a "search and replace" at the end—or leave the manuscript with some em dashes and some double hyphens. Being fastidious is nice, of course, but not always necessary in less formal situations.

Okay, let's discuss the "en" dash, which never used to be spoken of, except by typesetters. In fact, the current computer keyboard doesn't have an en dash (or an em dash), but the symbol can be found in your word processing program (probably—I can't guarantee that). In Word, we pull down the "Insert" menu and click on "Symbol," then "Special Characters" and select the en dash and double click.

An en dash is longer than a hyphen and shorter than an em dash. The en dash replaces the "to" in an expression showing a range of numbers or connection between numbers, items, times, and concepts: June–July, ages 10–18, New York–Washington, flatfooted– dyspeptic. An en dash also can be used in compound adjectives when one or more of the elements comprise more than one word (the Hilary Clinton–Bill Clinton marriage) or a hyphenated word (semi-automatic–semi-manual operation).

But when we come right down to it, the en dash is so specialized and so hard to even recognize in print that unless we want to be know-it-alls (these are just hyphens here), we simply ignore it. So, I had to tell you all this? I suppose it's better *I* tell you than it comes as a nasty surprise heard from a stranger.

Hyphens

Once upon a time, hyphens were used to break words between lines when we typed a manuscript using a typewriter. Yes, we humans ourselves decided where to put in the hyphen. We might even have stopped to look up a word in the dictionary to judge the syllable breaks.

These days, of course, no human hand would ever bend to any such task. The computer, when asked (nicely) to "justify" text—what is called flush left/flush right—will produce hyphenated words. Mostly we needn't think about the results, though once in a while the computer will goof and produce what is called a "bad break." Those of us who might be proofreading such a document can circle the bad break if we recognize it as such, and the person responsible for how the pages come out can try to fix the problem. Occasionally, however, the computer software will dig in its heels, as software sometimes does, and will make a bigger goof—maybe a big "hole" of space in the middle of the line—to compensate for the bad break. Such is the life.

In the 21st century, the hyphen is used primarily to create a compound adjective, an adjective-noun used as an adjective phrase, or a compound noun. The decision as to whether a noun takes a hyphen or not isn't ours, so use the dictionary. For more about hyphens, check out the chapter on adjectives and adverbs.

Apostrophes

The apostrophe indicates possession, creates contractions, shows the omission of numbers or letters, and creates plurals of letters, numbers, words, and symbols.

❖ *Possession:* The car is Herman's. That's James's ring. Don't touch the birds' nest. The Joneses' trees were trimmed today. He bought Jane and Judy's house. He was going to buy Nan's or Larry's house but changed his mind. The children's nanny went with them. We were in court every day of the six months' trial.

❖ *Contraction:* I'm going, and he's coming with me.

Watch the contractions because they might not mean what you want them to. For instance, "he's" means "he is" and shouldn't be used to mean "he was." Or, "Barbara's brought along to help with the paperwork" should be "Barbara is brought along..." because "Barbara's" is a possessive. Sometimes we can cheat, of course, but let's think twice.

❖ *Omissions:* 'Y'all hear? I'm goin' down the road for a burger.

The apostrophe before the "y" is the one standing in for the omission, as is the one in "goin'." The other two apostrophes create contractions.

❖ *Plurals:* He crosses through his 7's in the European fashion.

❖ The *and*'s in that sentence look funny to me.

We make a plural with an apostrophe only when we use the item as a "thing" without reference to its inherent meaning. The item itself may be placed in italic. By the way, we no longer seem to use an apostrophe when we say "the 1900s" and such. Ordinary plurals don't take an apostrophe (the Greens, the Jameses). We also use an apostrophe in pluralizing lower-case letters, but if we mean something other than the item as a thing, we don't use italic: Mind your p's and q's. (As opposed to: Mind how you write the *q*'s.)

Parentheses and Brackets

Parentheses introduce qualifying or explaining material. Really, they are similar to dashes—well, you can't have just one side of the parenthesis, whereas you can have a single dash. The word "parenthesis" stands for one of the symbols, however. The word for a pair of the symbols is "parentheses." Parentheses can surround an entire sentence with its end punctuation inside or can enclose only a word, phrase, list, or clause within a sentence. Parentheses are used to enclose an acronym or, oppositely, the full name of that which has been abbreviated, or a place name and such: *The Chicago Manual of Style* (*CMOS*); *CMOS* (*The Chicago Manual of Style*); Dr. Abraham Johnson (Lansing, MI).

❖ *Correct:* She wanted to (but couldn't) go to Europe that summer.

❖ *Correct:* She wanted to—but couldn't—go to Europe that summer.

❖ *Correct:* She wanted to, but couldn't, go to Europe that summer.

❖ *Correct:* Lilah (why did it always come back to Lilah?) started what no one else had the stomach to finish.

❖ *Correct:* Lilah—why did it always come back to Lilah?—started what no one else had the stomach to finish.

> ❖ *Incorrect:* Lilah, why did it always come back to Lilah?, started what no one else had the stomach to finish.

The parentheses and dashes each create a bit of a different sound, but are equally acceptable, as are commas, when they're appropriate. When do we capitalize a full sentence within parentheses? That depends. Partly, that depends on whose rules you follow. One set of rules states that a sentence in parentheses interrupting another sentence and that serves as a *question* or *exclamation* starts with a capital. So the above sentence would go: "Lilah (Why did it always come back to Lilah?) started what no one else had the stomach to finish." Under this set of rules, an *ordinary* sentence— one that ends with a period—in parentheses and interrupting another sentence begins with a lower case word (except when that first word is a proper noun). That, to me, really tops it for arcane ridiculousness.

I follow the other set of rules from *The Columbia Guide to Standard American English*, which says "inside a sentence, the materials within parentheses need not be capitalized..."

Brackets, also called "square brackets," are like parentheses. They are used in pairs only. They are used to enclose material added to a quote by the author who is quoting. And they are used inside parentheses to create a sort of inner parentheses.

Capitals

We capitalize sentences and the pronoun "I." We capitalize the word "God" when used to refer to the one God, which is the alpha and the omega, although to refer to a god, such as Zeus, we don't capitalize. We don't capitalize the seasons: winter, fall, autumn, summer, spring. We do capitalize the regions of the U.S. and words derived from the regions: the Northern states; her Southern accent; the Midwest; his Western boots.

We capitalize proper nouns, which include a whole load of stuff, from the names of countries and languages to the names of people and holidays.

We capitalize titles and relationship names only if they are used as names:

> ❖ *Correct:* I asked Aunt Agatha to bring Major Lynd to the party. The major has been a friend of my aunt's for many years. She calls him "Major," as if that were his name, although I happen to know that his name is "John." Apparently John once thought he would become a general, General Lynd, and he believed he might later run for president of the United States. My aunt told my mother all of that, and I told Mother not to repeat it as the story made the major sound ridiculous.

Again, if you don't know in regard to a particular word whether we capitalize, use the dictionary.

> ❖ *Incorrect:* The colonel made a quick u-turn with her Fiat.
>
> ❖ *Correct:* The colonel made a quick U-turn with her Fiat.

Bold Type

Generally speaking, we don't use bold type in ordinary text. We do use bold for headlines and subheads. (I discussed the use of italics in the chapter on how we use quote marks.)

* I would like to thank my parents, Ann Rand and God for helping me.... "Quite a set of parents, wouldn't you say?" asks copy editor Linda M DeVore, who can be found at https://grammarnow.com.

Exercise

Punctuate the following:

its funny how you can think better sometimes in motion and while hitting those balls with my new stainless steel putting iron I contemplated the most memorable case I'd really ever been involved with but that of course had been long before I'd gone in for the law had been a real life prosecutor and had consequently been elected to hear the trials and tribulations that poured forth endlessly from baxter county the circumstance I meditated on as I often did was something that had happened during the war while I was a prisoner of the Japanese held under unimaginable conditions among a pack of wretched starving disease ridden soldiers deserted by their country on the philippine island of panay as ms roberts says in our course text when trying to identify in which mystery subgenre you want to write a first consideration is who your sleuth will be she sets forth to identify the various sleuths as follows the amateur everyman or everywoman who stumbles onto the scene the semi pro journalist lawyer insurance investigator the private investigator from the early cliched hard hitting guy in a trench coat to the real and licensed type and the police which will actually include law enforcement of many types each kind of sleuth can express a range of tones and experience degrees of violence further contributing to the characterization of the specific subgenre

Quiz

1. If we start a sentence with a coordinating conjunction, such as an "and" or a "but," how do we punctuate that?
2. Do we use commas for direct address only in quotes?
3. What is an "interrupting phrase"?
4. Do we use commas to set off an interrupting phrase?
5. Do we use commas to set off an introductory phrase?
6. Do we use a comma to set off participle phrases?
7. Would we use a comma to set off an introductory or interrupting adverb clause?
8. Do we use a comma after a single introductory word?
9. What's a "Harvard" comma?
10. What punctuation does a series of clauses take?
11. May we use a comma inside parentheses?
12. Do we use a comma with "restrictive" material?
13. Does a "which" take a comma before it?
14. May we use commas whenever we like?
15. Should we have a question mark or exclamation mark only at the end of a sentence?
16. Where are semicolons used?
17. What does a colon do?

*Claim your free access to **www.firstwriter.com**: See p.263*

18. What's an "em dash"?
19. Do em dashes differ in use from parentheses?
20. What is the primary use of the hyphen?
21. What are the four uses of the apostrophe?
22. Mark the following as correct or incorrect: On the West side of town, the Southern states, the Hospital building, Mt. Sinai Hospital, the Convent, the 18th Century, aunt Agatha, my Aunt, the General, General Eisenhower.

Answers

Exercise:

As I wrote the pieces, I'm the one who punctuated them here. However, your punctuation might be different from mine and still be correct.

It's funny how you can think better sometimes in motion, and while hitting those balls with my new stainless steel putting iron, I contemplated the most memorable case I'd really ever been involved with. But that, of course, had been long before I'd gone in for the law, had been a real-life prosecutor, and had consequently been elected to hear the trials and tribulations that poured forth endlessly from Baxter County. The circumstance I meditated on, as I often did, was something that had happened during the war while I was a prisoner of the Japanese, held under unimaginable conditions among a pack of wretched, starving, disease-ridden soldiers deserted by their country on the Philippine island of Panay.

As Ms. Roberts says in our course text, when trying to identify in which mystery subgenre you want to write, "A first consideration is who your sleuth will be." She sets forth to identify the various sleuths as follows: the amateur (everyman or everywoman who stumbles onto the scene); the semi-pro (journalist, lawyer, insurance investigator); the private investigator (from the early clichéd, hard-hitting guy in a trench coat, to the real and licensed type); and the police (which will actually include law enforcement of many types). Each kind of sleuth can express a range of tones and experience degrees of violence, further contributing to the characterization of the specific subgenre.

Quiz:

1. If we start a sentence with a coordinating conjunction, such as an "and" or a "but," how do we punctuate that?
We don't actually have to use any punctuation at that point, although from time to time we might use a comma after the "and" or the "but."

2. Do we use commas for direct address only in quotes?
Well, yes. Except for silent speech, that's the only place we employ direct address. We insert a comma on both sides of the noun (proper or common) used for the direct address.

3. What is an interrupting phrase?
An interrupting phrase is one out of its linear or expected position.

4. Do we use commas to set off an interrupting phrase?
We use commas to set off interrupting adjective phrases; sometimes we use commas to set off interrupting adverb phrases.

5. Do we use commas to set off an introductory phrase?
If we choose to, though when the phrases are more than four or five words long, we usually do.

6. Do we use a comma to set off participle phrases?
When the participle phrase is an introductory phrase, yes, we do. When the participle phrase is in its expected position, we may or may not use the comma or comma pair.

7. Would we use a comma to set off an introductory or interrupting adverb clause?
Yes. But we must be aware of the difference between a phrase and a clause.

8. Do we use a comma after a single introductory word?
We often do, but may choose not to.

9. What's a "Harvard" comma?
The Harvard comma, also known as the "serial" comma, is the comma before the "and" in a list. The use of this comma is suggested for clarity's sake.

10. What punctuation does a series of clauses take?
A series of clauses—even dependent ones—with internal punctuation or that are long or complex will take semicolons. A series of short clauses may be punctuated using a series of commas.

11. May we use a comma inside parentheses?
This is a trick question. Of course we may, if the comma is required by the contents. But we may not use a comma right before the end parenthesis.

12. Do we use a comma with "restrictive" material?
No. Restrictive means no comma because we need the identifiers that explain the noun or pronoun being discussed.

13. Does a "which" take a comma before it?
In general, yes, when the "which" is used to open a nonrestrictive modifier. The "which" can also be used instead of a "that" in a sentence that already has a "that," in which case, the comma will not be used. "Which" is also used in other ways that don't require a comma, such as in the prepositional phrase "in which case."

14. May we use commas whenever we like?
We must follow the comma "don'ts," but we can use optional commas if we like and can use commas for clarity and deliberate pauses if they don't violate the "don'ts."

15. Should we have a question mark or exclamation mark only at the end of a sentence?
We can have either mark in the middle of the sentence if the use is otherwise appropriate.

16. Where are semicolons used?
They're used between independent clauses and between complex elements of a list.

17. What does a colon do?
A colon announces that something related to the phrase or clause is coming immediately after the punctuation mark.

18. What's an "em dash"?
An "em dash" is the long dash we use to introduce "asides."

19. Do em dashes differ in use from parentheses?
They are similar and sometimes may be used interchangeably. Parentheses present the material a bit more "quietly."

20. What is the primary use of the hyphen?
The primary use of the hyphen is to create a compound adjective or adjective-noun.

21. What are the four uses of the apostrophe?
To show possession, to form a contraction, to show missing

letters, to show some limited types of plurals.

22. Mark the following as correct or incorrect: On the West side of town, the Southern states, the Hospital building, Mt. Sinai Hospital, the Convent, the 18th Century, aunt Agatha, my Aunt, the General, General Eisenhower.

On the West side of town (incorrect—we only capitalize regions of the United States unless local convention suggests we capitalize parts of a city), the Southern states (correct), the Hospital building (incorrect), Mt. Sinai Hospital (correct—we capitalize exact names of hospitals), the Convent (incorrect), the 18th Century (incorrect—we don't capitalize the centuries), aunt Agatha (incorrect—we capitalize names and we're using "Aunt" as part of her name), my Aunt (incorrect), the General (incorrect), General Eisenhower (correct).

Get Free Access to the firstwriter.com Website

Once you've written your novel or short story, you'll need to find markets such as publishers, agents, and magazines to which you can pitch your work. To help you, this book allows you to access the firstwriter.com website for up to three months for free.

To claim your free access to the firstwriter.com website simply go to the website at https://www.firstwriter.com/subscribe and begin the subscription process as normal. On the second page, enter the required details (such as your name and address, etc.) then for "Voucher/coupon number" enter the following code:

- **NK79-WR21**

This will reduce the cost of creating a subscription by up to $15/£10/€15, making it free to create a monthly, quarterly, or combination subscription. Alternatively, you can use the discount to take out an annual or life subscription at a reduced rate.

Continue the process until your account is created. Please note that you will need to provide your payment details, even if there is no up-front payment. This is in case you choose to leave your subscription running after the free initial period, but there is no obligation for you to do so.

When you use this code to take out a free subscription you are under no obligation to make any payments whatsoever and you are free to cancel your account before you make any payments if you wish.

If you need any assistance, please email:

- support@firstwriter.com.

If you have found this book useful, please consider leaving a review on the website where you bought it!

What You Get

Once you have set up access to the site you will be able to benefit from all the following features:

Databases

All our databases are updated almost every day, and include powerful search facilities to help you find exactly what you need. Searches that used to take you hours or even days in print books or on search engines can now be done in seconds, and produce more accurate and up-to-date information. Our agents database also includes independent reports from at least three separate sources, showing you which are the top agencies and helping you avoid the scams that are all over the internet. You can try out any of our databases before you subscribe:

- Search dozens of **current competitions**
- Search **over 2,300 magazines**
- Search **over 650 literary agencies**
- Search **over 1,900 book publishers** that **don't** charge fees

PLUS advanced features to help you with your search:

- Save searches and save time – set up to 15 search parameters specific to your work, save them, and then access the search results with a single click whenever you log in. You can even save multiple different searches if you have different types of work you are looking to place.

- Add personal notes to listings, visible only to you and fully searchable – helping you to organise your actions.

- Set reminders on listings to notify you when to submit your work, when to follow up, when to expect a reply, or any other custom action.

- Track which listings you've viewed and when, to help you organise your search – any listings which have changed since you last viewed them will be highlighted for your attention.

Daily email updates

As a subscriber you will be able to take advantage of our email alert service, meaning you can specify your particular interests and we'll send you automatic email updates when we change or add a listing that matches them. So if you're interested in agents dealing in mystery in the United States you can have us send you emails with the latest updates about them – keeping you up to date without even having to log in.

User feedback

Our agent, publisher, and magazine databases all include a user feedback feature that allows our subscribers to leave feedback on each listing – giving you not only the chance to have your say about the markets you contact, but giving a unique authors' perspective on the listings.

Save on copyright protection fees

If you're sending your work away to publishers, competitions, or literary agents, it's vital that you first protect your copyright. As a subscriber to firstwriter.com you can do this through our site and save 10% on the copyright registration fees normally payable for protecting your work internationally through the Intellectual Property Rights Office.

Monthly newsletter

When you subscribe to firstwriter.com you also receive our monthly email newsletter – described by one publishing company as "the best in the business" – including articles, news, and interviews for writers. And the best part is that you can continue to receive the newsletter even after you stop your paid subscription – at no cost!

Terms and Conditions

The promotional code contained in this publication may be used by the owner of the book only to create one subscription to firstwriter.com at a reduced cost, or for free. It may not be used by or disseminated to third parties. Should the code be misused then the owner of the book will be liable for any costs incurred, including but not limited to payment in full at the standard rate for the subscription in question or any additional subscriptions. The code may be redeemed against the creation of a new account only – it cannot be redeemed against the ongoing costs of keeping a subscription open. In order to create a subscription a method of payment must be provided, but there is no obligation to make any payment. Subscriptions may be cancelled at any time, and if an account is cancelled before any payment becomes due then no payment will be made. Once a subscription has been created, the normal schedule of payments will begin on a monthly, quarterly, or annual basis, unless a life Subscription is selected, or the subscription is cancelled prior to the first payment becoming due. Subscriptions may be cancelled at any time, but if they are left open beyond the date at which the first payment becomes due and is processed then payments will not be refundable.